PRAISE FOR THIS BOOK

"In *The Cosmic Christ and The Concrete Jesus: Mystics, The Black Prophetic Tradition, and Why I'm Still a Christian*, Kevin Sweeney invites us to see Jesus in everyone, to embody His heart and compassion for the marginalized, and to follow Him more deeply as the source of liberation and love."

— **Dr. Terence Lester, Founder of Love Beyond Walls and Author of *I See You*, *When We Stand*, and *All God's Children***

"In *The Cosmic Christ and the Concrete Jesus*, Kevin Sweeney invites us to set aside everything we thought we knew about religion, Christianity, and Jesus and to, instead, reimagine our understanding of love. Love as a concept. Love as a practice. Love as the embodiment of liberation. Kevin is the ideal guide, gentle yet fearless, as he walks us straight through the heart of investigating our faith, reexamining our definition of justice, and reevaluating our attachment to the conventional framing of the American narrative. This book will invite you to be honest, to reflect, and do the work to repair as you find your faith anew, exchanging what has kept you stuck for a way of life in the flow of equitable, reparative, unconditional love for yourself and all of humanity."

— **Sarah Carter, Co-author of *Slow Burn: Reclaiming Yourself After Everything Burns to the Ground***

"This book is so good that I have to use unlikely pairs of words to describe it: majestic and practical, profound and simple, revolutionary and peaceful, transformative and uplifting, cosmic and concrete. If you're dissatisfied with most popular versions of Christian faith today, you owe yourself this book to help you in your rethinking process. Big thanks to Kevin Sweeney!

— **Brian D. McLaren, author of *Do I Stay Christian?***

"Kevin Sweeney's *The Cosmic Christ and The Concrete Jesus* masterfully bridges personal spirituality and holistic justice. Sweeney invites readers to embrace the infinite love of the Cosmic Christ and follow the justice-driven path of the Concrete Jesus. This book is a powerful call to embody a faith that is both deeply contemplative and actively engaged in confronting injustice. A must-read for those seeking a transformative and action-oriented spirituality."

— **Brandan Robertson, Author of *Queer and Christian: Reclaiming Our Bible, Our Faith, and Our Place at the Table***

"Truth is liberating. This book is a truth sermon! Be set free."

— **Dr. Ralph Basui Watkins, MFA, DMin, PhD, Peachtree Professor of Evangelism and Church Growth, Columbia Theological Seminary**

"I am a white former evangelical pastor, and the Black liberation tradition has been pivotal in helping me hold on to my faith in Jesus while learning how to follow him in a world still dominated by oppressive powers. Many of us who have begun to deconstruct the fear-based versions of Christianity often find ourselves grappling with uncertainty—wondering what, if anything, Christianity can still offer us. In this book, Kevin shows us that the Christian tradition can still be a powerful pathway into a deeper connection with God and an active role in the ongoing struggle for collective liberation. What sets Kevin's work apart is the way he brings together the often-separated paths of mystical encounter with God and social justice. Rather than pitting these two as opposing forces, Kevin weaves them into a coherent, compelling vision for why Christian spirituality can still be a vital, life-giving pathway. This book not only responds to the challenges many face in deconstructing old frameworks but also invites us to rediscover a version of Christianity that is centered in love, liberation, and transformative action—on both a personal and societal scale."

— **Brian Recker, Host of the *Sacred Counsel* podcast**

KEVIN SWEENEY

THE
COSMIC
CHRIST
AND THE
CONCRETE
JESUS

MYSTICS, THE BLACK
PROPHETIC TRADITION, AND
WHY I'M STILL A CHRISTIAN

Copyright © 2025 by Kevin Sweeney
First Edition

THE HOLY BIBLE, NEW INTERNATIONAL VERSION®, NIV® Copyright © 1973, 1978, 1984, 2011 by Biblica, Inc.® Used by permission. All rights reserved worldwide.

Cover Image and Design by Larry Ganiron
Interior Layout by Matthew J. Distefano

PRINT ISBN 978-1-964252-40-7
ELECTRONIC ISBN 978-1-964252-41-4
Printed in the United States of America

QUOIR

Published by Quoir
Chico, California
www.quoir.com

CONTENTS

*For every person following Jesus toward justice,
and quietly experiencing the fullness of Christ.
The Kingdom is yours.*

ACKNOWLEDGMENTS

Christine: Thank you for holding it all together.

Mikayla: My superstar. I see you and I'm always with you.

True: My big dog. Always keep going.

Larry: Thank you for creating a visual language for my voice.

The Great Mystics: For always trusting what you see.

The Black Prophetic Tradition: For speaking the truth in a culture that is never ready to hear it.

My Hospice Patients: For seeing me with the eyes of Christ.

My Quoir Fam: For creating a space for writers who thought they might never have one.

INTRODUCTION

This book is about making sense of two seemingly separate stories in my life.

One of these moments is me in my mid twenties sitting on the edge of a cliff in prayer, over looking The Back Bay, in Orange County, CA. In this story I was by myself, sitting in silence, invisible to the rest of the world, quietly responding with a "yes" to the Divine "Yes" that has been echoing for eternity.

It was here I would welcome my small but sacred place in Christ.

Breath.

Love.

Grace.

Safety.

Connection.

Embrace.

It was humbly receiving from God everything our false self wants to fight for from others.

The other moment was me in my late twenties marching through the streets of Downtown Los Angeles with a collective of protesters exposing the unjust murder of Trayvon Martin. In this story I am marching with others, consciously making noise, visible to the world, and defiantly saying a collective "no" to the injustice and brutality towards Black people that has been present in this country since its inception.

It was here I would continue to receive my small place in the movement toward the vision of justice that Jesus lived and died for two thousand years ago.

Liberation.

Action.

Organizing.

Witness.

Demonstration.

Embodied.

It was boldly challenging the institutionalized white supremacy in our country that an unconscionable amount of people are still too comfortable with.

The connection between these two stories and the relationship between these two moments is what this book is about.

The first was about falling into the infinite embrace of the Cosmic Christ, the other was about following the liberating path of the Concrete Jesus. This offering is about the unbreakable link between both.

What do I mean by the Cosmic Christ and the Concrete Jesus?

Well,

let's begin with The Cosmic Christ.

What is the name for that which holds all things together? What do you call the substance of the Self that is beneath and in every individual self? How do you describe the energetic presence that is born within, yet alway remains beyond? How can you put into words the gravitational pull of the future that is also the sacred ground of the present?

And is there a connecting name for the diversity of expressions of this Living Reality in the Scriptures?

The God who spoke life into existence in Genesis 1. The Spirit that breathed life into humanity in Genesis 2. The Force that holds all thing together in Colossians 1. The God who was connected with the poets who had never heard of Jesus in Acts 17. The Divinity that was fully embodied through the humanity of Jesus in the gospels.

The unifying name used by some of the great mystics for this source is The Cosmic Christ.

Beginning in the very beginning with the Big Bang, through atoms, molecules, cells, simple organisms, to human beings, and the formation of communities, there has been a hidden evolutionary force at work driving this sacred process. From the depths of human creativity, through the unfolding of culture, to the expanding universe, and behind the curtain of the cosmic drama playing out as life itself, there is something good and powerful intentionally working.

This is the Cosmic Christ.

Christ has been unfolding in, through, and as the universe since the very beginning. The Cosmic Christ is the creative drive of evolution itself, the organizing principle within all forms of complexity, and the transcendent power immanent within all of life.

The Cosmic Christ is the name for everything that matters, and for the depth of matter itself. It is the ever present Presence that grounds us, holds us, and loves us through life. This is the source of joy, the ground of peace, the space within which all of life arises and the substance of the arising as well.

Which is why Richard Rohr says that Christ is "another name for everything."

I want you to know how to see the face of the Cosmic Christ everywhere and to trust your place within the center of her heart.

So we are welcomed to surrender to the Cosmic Christ, but we also are invited to follow the Concrete Jesus.

Now, a bit about the Concrete Jesus.

Actually in order to make more sense of the nature of the Concrete Jesus, first, it will be helpful to take a contrasting look at the abstract Jesus most people are familiar with.

I am not sure if you are aware of this, but there is an abstract white Jesus that has a tremendous amount of influence in our country. This Jesus tends to side with those in power, is mostly apolitical, and miraculously transforms all radical social acts in the gospels into cute little nuggets of wisdom for our individual lives today.

Have you ever met him or heard about him before?

Of course you have. He's everywhere!

You know? The guy who has been completely extracted from his social and political context in ancient Palestine, and has become a mascot for white Christian nationalism in the United States. You know who I'm talking about. He's not a big fan of the poor, has virtually nothing to say about oppression, and is mostly concerned with eternal salvation or personal piety.

Yes, exactly.

The one preached about in most churches each and every Sunday morning.

In case you are still having a hard time recognizing this figure, here's a couple examples of how this abstract Jesus manifests in real time.

When people are more concerned with whether or not you believe in original sin than confronting the original sin of slavery and the oppression of indigenous people in our country, you can be sure the abstract white Jesus is afoot.

Or if a church is passionate about providing charity for the underprivileged, while completely ignoring the social structures that have established a system that creates under and over privileged people, you know the abstract white Jesus is present.

And when you have pastors who have preached hundreds of sermons about how the inclusivity of Jesus in the gospels always offended the religious status quo, while continuously getting upset when other followers of Jesus include LGBTQ+ people in their churches, the abstract white Jesus is definitely at work.

Now, you know exactly who I am talking about.

But thankfully.

This is not the only Jesus that I have ever known.

Now, to the Concrete Jesus.

There is a concrete and liberating Jesus that has been proclaimed by the Black Prophetic Christian tradition in the United States, and that has grounded my faith for the past fifteen years.

This is an earthy and embodied Jesus whose ministry is defined by his identification with the marginalized and solidarity with the oppressed. A socially engaged Jesus who laughed at the power of empire, told stories about the impotency of status and wealth, and confronted an entire predatory economic system with the flip of a table.

This is the Concrete Jesus whose compassion to the poor challenged the indifference of the rich. The Jesus whose emancipatory and controversial sermons almost got him killed by his own people. The incarnational savior and rebel who disrupted the status quo, was seen as a threat to the religious and political authorities, and who was ultimately crucified as an enemy of the state.

This is the Jesus that inspired Dr. James Cone to write, "God was the God of history, the Liberator of the oppressed from bondage. Jesus was not an abstract Word of God, but God's Word made flesh who came to set the prisoner free."

The Concrete Jesus had his feet on the ground, his heart with the oppressed, and his eyes fixed on structures and systems that were getting in the way of life. This is the liberating Jesus of the Black prophetic tradition, and this is the Jesus that creates the contours of the way I have given my life to.

So there is the Cosmic Christ and the Concrete Jesus.

And in this book, I want you to feel what I mean when I write about the relationship between the Cosmic Christ and the Concrete Jesus.

I want you to see how the power of the Big Bang and the presence of the boundary breaking Jesus are the same.

I want you to see that the universal Source of love and the Substance of liberation are One.

I want you to see that the God who has no edges also takes sides in situations of injustice.

And why are the mystics and the Black prophetic tradition my guides? Because in my own journey, the mystics gave me the Cosmic Christ, and the Black prophetic tradition has given me the Concrete Jesus.

It's actually that simple. And although these different streams are what help me live into the flow of God personally, I also believe they have the power to invite all of us into this fullness of God universally.

My hope is that you experience the love of the Cosmic Christ who tells us that we are safe, and to hear the voice of the Concrete Jesus who calls us to be dangerous.

And if I'm honest, a part of this work is making sense of why I'm still a Christian. After my initial awakening in Christ twenty years ago, and the steady flow of evolution and transformation since then, I wonder why is it still so natural and comfortable for me to be so committed to the way of Jesus?

I've read all the books that will make someone question their beliefs about Jesus and their participation in the Christian tradition. I've wrestled with the radical contingency of everything to the point that it leaves you unable to hold onto anything with a hundred percent certainty, and yet somehow I am still just as committed to this path as I was when I was first "on fire" for Jesus two decades ago.

Maybe it's because from my initial awakening, my faith was not based on beliefs, but on embodiment and experience. So, as beliefs about God, Jesus, and the Bible changed for me over the years, my place in the experiential center of Christ remained unmoved.

Or maybe it's my awareness that what is commonly called deconstruction right now for Christians, is simply the movement from one stage of consciousness to the next. And thankfully, there are all of these developmental models that enable us to see that the deconstruction that feels so catastrophic while it's happening is merely one evolutionary step on a spiritual path that keeps going.

For most religious people, beliefs are a house for their ego. So when they start to deconstruct their beliefs, it feels like they are dismantling their home and their life. Which is one reason why it feels so traumatic.

For me, this wasn't the case because faith was not beliefs I had about God, it was the experiential knowing of God. So as my beliefs changed and evolved over the years, it did not feel like taking apart my home, it registered more like updating the map while traveling on the terrain. And updating the map as you explore and discover more on the terrain of Christ is natural and necessary.

So, during a time when doubt and deconstruction seem to be making all of the headlines, it is my desire for people to not only see why I'm still a Christian, but to see all of the life in Christ beyond their own movement through new stages of faith. I hope that people will not only change their beliefs, but re-imagine a faith that is not defined by what you believe, but how well you are loved.

Which is why I can say yes.

Yes to the doubting of certainty.

Yes to the critiques of Christian nationalism.

Yes to the challenging of exclusivity and rejection of LGBTQ+ people.

Yes to the accountability of the institutional abuse of power in the church.

Yes to the dismantling of white supremacy and patriarchy.

Yes to the letting go of the Bible as an inerrant handbook.

Yes to being honest about the trauma you experienced from religion.

Yes to these and every other legitimate reason to leave behind the Jesus you were handed and the faith and church that is no longer working.

Yes! Yes! Yes!

But after the anger, oppositional energy and being clear of what you are not, then what? Where do we go? Who do we become? How do we keep moving toward wholeness? What does it mean to be a person of faith? What do we give our lives to?

And even more specifically, how do we remain a Christian?

After waking up and beginning to move beyond these boundaries and false limitations that have been placed on us, there is still a whole life that needs to be lived. My identification with the Cosmic Christ and commitment to the Concrete Jesus communicate what that path feels like for me, and hopeful provides some light for what that path might feel like for you.

I want to add one interesting observation I had while I was writing this book.

You can be fully committed to the way of Jesus regardless of your religious beliefs.

I know that sounds weird.

But life in the living reality of Christ is before belief, beyond belief, and can never be contained within beliefs.

Wrestling with why I am still a Christian and the recognition that you can know God's love and work for liberation in this world without having to hold any specific abstract beliefs about God are directly connected for me.

Dogma does not qualify you or disqualify you from love.

Doctrine does not determine the depth of your experience of being known by God.

Holding abstract beliefs about Jesus are not required to follow Jesus.

Paul's transformative encounter with the resurrected Christ was before belief. The defining experience Jacob had while wrestling and fighting with God was beyond belief. The father in the gospel of Mark saying to Jesus, "I do believe, help me overcome my unbelief" communicates a form of faith with Jesus that is not limited by the beliefs we carry.

For me, a belief is valuable insofar as it becomes a path to embodiment. And if any religious belief is not embodied and grounded in our lived reality of love and liberation, it does not matter.

Isn't that what the incarnation of Jesus was about?

There is a great relief and sense of freedom when you can see that we can be One with Christ and totally committed to the way of Jesus without the baggage of doctrine, or the need to dogmatically carry hollow beliefs.

And I hope my observation about beliefs is actually an invitation.

The invitation is that your beliefs can change, you can even lose your beliefs, and still be beautifully in tune with the energy of Christ and devoted to the path of Jesus. Even when the structure of belief you held falls apart, the substance of Christ will still hold you together.

So now, let's talk more about the liberating Jesus.

ONE

The Concrete Jesus

When I graduated from Fuller Seminary in the Spring of 2012, my name was called and I walked across the stage to shake the president's hand and receive my diploma. Right before I heard my name, I slipped my copy of James Cone's book "Black Theology and Black Power" out of my robe, and held it up on display for the audience to see as I walked across to approach the president.

As I came face to face with the one responsible for giving me my diploma, he looked down at the book, I switched it to my other hand so we could embrace, and I smiled as he wished me well and said congratulations.

Sure, a couple of hours before this during an informational meeting about the ceremony, one of the organizers explicitly told us we were not allowed to flash anything on stage as we walked across. But the thing is that I already had my copy of Cone's book in my waist band and had been planning this for weeks.

Friends.

Family.

A room filled with people proud and excited that someone they know and love is getting ready for their unique path of proclaiming the good news of Jesus Christ.

And there I was walking and smiling while holding a copy of "Black Theology and Black Power," getting ready to hold it up for everyone at the ceremony to see.

What exactly was happening here?

What was I trying to say?

Why would a young white male walk across a stage to receive his graduate degree from an historical seminary, holding a copy of a book titled, "Black Theology and Black Power?"

Well.

That book was a critique of the institutionalized white supremacy that had been embedded in this school since its inception. It was a challenge to the eurocentricity invisibly flowing (to those in privilege) through the courses, curriculum, and resources that they deemed central for Christian formation.

Cone's groundbreaking legacy represented a corrective to the marginalization of the voices of Black people specifically, and marginalized thinkers in general at this seminary, and in every white church and religious institution in The United States of America.

Yes, this moment was about Fuller Theological Seminary.

But it was bigger than just Fuller. (And by the way, I loved my experience at this school.)

It was a confrontation with the slave holding Christianity that tragically defined so much of the church, and the United States of America's experiment with democracy.

It was a challenge to the heart of a Christian faith that empowered countless white people to witness the lynching of a Black body on a Thursday afternoon and feel comfortable at a church on a Sunday morning.

It was a critique of the white churches and clergy who either actively resisted the civil rights movement, or passively watched as Black folks were catching hell in this country during an era that many white people still want to go back to.

It was an unsettling of the imagination that still allows white Christians to continue to show up on Sundays and sing love songs to Jesus while being indifferent to, or worse, antagonistic toward the ongoing legacy and murder of Black people by police in our country.

James Cone taught me that liberation is the heart of the gospel of Jesus.

Kelly Brown Douglas showed me that Jesus' concrete life was defined by his identification with the marginalized and his solidarity with the oppressed.

The prophetic Black Christian tradition enabled me to see that following Jesus is not just about uplifting hearts, but about tearing down broken systems.

Walking across that stage with Cone's words in my hands was me saying that without the status quo challenging, system confronting, and liberating Jesus that was given to me by the Black prophetic tradition, I do not have the whole Jesus.

Without this liberating Jesus, we are left with an abstract, white savior that is powerless in the face of real evil and concrete injustice, and a truncated and destructive version of the gospel.

Andre Henry wrote, "...I'd conclude that White Jesus was standing in the way of the revolution, and that realization made me seriously wrestle with questions about the role that spirituality, religion, and the divine have in the revolution for justice."

While referring to white people not taking liberation seriously, Dante Stewart said, "They never had any need to do that. America worked well for them."

Candice Benbow wrote that, "White scholars weren't making room in their scholarship to discuss the treatment of Black people."

What I hear from these Black voices is that the privilege and power of whiteness in America has not required or enabled white theologians and Christians to see the truth of the Black experience in America. And as a result, have been prevented from grasping the depths of oppression present in the Black experience, which has then made it impossible to have compassion toward Black people.

And to extend this further, this blindness has not only made it improbable for white Christians to see the equality and sacredness of Black people, it has made it impossible to see the multidimensional nature of Jesus' ministry.

Whiteness does not see the need for liberation, does not cry out for liberation, and therefore does not have the ability to lead us to liberation. And since this white Jesus does not have the power to lead us to liberation, he has actually has become a barrier to a Christ-shaped revolution and divine justice.

This is why we need a more concrete and liberating Jesus.

A Jesus embedded in the struggle of people on the edges of society.

A Jesus whose proximity to the oppressed forced him to feel the need for liberation.

A Jesus whose divine impulse is not to align with the powerful, but empower the marginalized.

Many years ago, the Black prophetic tradition awakened me to the revolutionary nature of this Concrete Jesus. Without the voices of Black women within this tradition I would not have the vision of the status quo challenging and liberating Jesus I am still committed to today. Furthermore, without a Queer imagination from within this tradition, I would not have the clarity to require the full inclusion of LGBTQ+ people in the church and the fight for their equality in our country as an integral part of my understanding of justice and Jesus.

It is very simple.

The abstract white Jesus within most churches will not lead us to a future that is shaped by the justice of God because those who have been in need of liberation are the ones who are going to lead us to liberation.

There is a disturbing and enlightening scene from the television show Roots of a slave master reading his Bible. While he is sitting on his veranda reading the Scriptures, overlooking a massive cotton field filled with enslaved Black people, he is involved in an interesting conversation with one of the older slaves about mercy.

The older slave was pleading with his master to extend mercy to one of the younger slaves. While barely even looking at the slave calling for mercy, the master refuses to relent, and is unwilling to hear this cry for leniency. His will remains strong, his heart remains closed, and he is unable to see the humanity of this man and others like him. And what is most revealing is this entire conversation was taking place on a plantation defined by the dehumanizing practice of slaveholding while the master is reading his Bible.

He was reading the Bible but could not see the humanity of Black people.

He was committed to Jesus but was completely comfortable with the brutalization of Black bodies.

He was familiar with the prophets but was ignorant to his own participation in and perpetuation of systems of injustice, violence, and greed.

This man could not see

But Kevin.

That was hundreds of years ago. This kind of blindness to the sacredness of all people has surely been left in the past where it belongs.

Maybe.

To a degree.

Or perhaps it has simply changed forms.

I was a part of an evangelical church in a suburban area in my 20s. I met some of my best friends there, learned how to lead groups, and even preached a little at the end. I was never on staff and knew I couldn't be a part of that church long term for my own sense of alignment, but I had a good experience overall.

It was also very conservative, conventional, and predominantly white. Bringing up Black or liberation theology in that context would be met with mostly surprise or resistance. I never heard anyone talk about institutionalized white supremacy, systemic racism, or the need to listen to the oppressed in order to gain access to deeper dimensions of the good news of Jesus.

No one ever mentioned the sins of the system of mass incarceration or the need to dismantle the prison industrial complex. There were never panels focused on the ways in which white supremacy was embedded within the systems of education, housing, and health care in our country. No classes were taught about how whiteness, power, and privilege can prevent us from seeing central themes in the Bible, such as liberation.

When it came to the historical oppression and unjust suffering of Black people in our country, it wasn't always antagonism that was at work, it was indifference.

Danté Stewart, while reflecting on the social situation of white people in the U.S, wrote, "It was that the idea of freedom and liberation didn't come from them, because for them and their children, they were safe, secure, and loved in a country built for them, that protected them, and desired their futures as much as they desired their comfort. They were already free. It was an abstract principle..."

Which raises a question.

How could we assume the collective voice of Christian leaders committed to following the abstract white Jesus, have the capacity to lead to liberation beyond the oppressive boundaries of the very system that works so well for them?

I remember having these unsettling moments in worship or communal life that would make me silently say, "people in this room really do not seem to care about the oppression of Black people in our country."

While they raise their hands in worship, they are not aware of the ways in which this entire political system has been leveraged against Black life from the beginning. While they attend small groups together, they do not see how their conservative views uncritically support and reinforce the very political structures of whiteness that maintain this oppression and marginalization today. While they feel totally safe walking the streets of their city, they definitely do not understand how the institutionalized white supremacy embedded in housing structures is what helped create the homogenous suburb that they are living in today.

Like the slave master sitting on the porch with his Bible, they could not see.

And the broader problem is not that these particular white people did not see or care about the oppression of Black people in the U.S., it is that the abstract white Jesus present in their church does not require them to care about social oppression and liberation at all as Christians.

But it is so enlightening to see that there is a consistent thread through out Scripture that reveals how we need the eyes of the Other to helps us see the truth out of our own.

In Acts 10, Peter needed Cornelius and his family to see that God's Spirit gives herself freely to all people.

In Acts 15, the Jerusalem Church needed the Gentiles' stories to embrace the universal accessibility of God.

Even Jesus, in Mark 7, seemed to need the persistence and perspective of the Syrophoenecian woman in order to express a wider dimension of divine healing.

So here's the thing.

We need the witness of Black people in our country to help us see.

We need the voices of liberation from the Black prophetic tradition to help us see the liberating nature of Jesus with clarity.

We need the voices of Queer Black leaders to expand our vision of justice to include the full embrace and welcome of our LGBTQ+ siblings.

Without the liberating Jesus that is given to us so powerfully from the Black prophetic tradition, we are left with the abstract white Jesus that does not have the vision or the power needed to lead us toward justice through the concrete realities of our times.

Without the liberating and Concrete Jesus,

we can be a Christian without caring about the marginalized,

we can be "saved" without being concerned about justice,

and we can believe in Christianity without actually becoming a Christian.

Having the structure of Christian belief without the substance of liberation is like having a well manufactured container without anything in it. Believing in the abstract Jesus of faith without a vision of and a commitment to the liberating Jesus of the gospels is like having a plan for a battle without ever daring to step foot on the battlefield.

It is a body with no heart.

It is a plane with no engine.

It is a box with no...well...you get the point.

So when I say that we need the liberating Black Jesus in order to see and embody a more holistic version of the gospel, what does this actually mean?

While this book itself is merely one answer to that question, here are the three main themes I carry from the Black prophetic tradition that have shaped my understanding of Jesus.

(1) The gospel is about liberation.

(2) Jesus' earthly ministry was defined by his solidarity with the oppressed and identification with the marginalized.

(3) The good news is not just about uplifting broken hearts it's about tearing down broken systems.

Without these three beliefs, we do not have the whole Jesus. And without some versions of these three themes integrated into a vision of the way of Jesus, I do not believe anyone can have the whole Jesus either.

Although these values will manifest and emerge naturally through each and every chapter of this book, let's begin by looking at each one of these in a bit more detail.

First. Liberation.

Without a commitment to liberation, we do not have the whole gospel.

I do not think I can be more clear than that.

We can have allegiance to a system of belief. We can have a personal devotion to God. We can even be considered orthodox in a confessional form of Christian faith. But without seeing the need for liberation from social, political, economic, or any other unjust structures, we cannot embody the fullness of the way of Jesus.

The pioneer of Black Theology James Cone wrote "In Black theology, liberation is the gospel and is not secondary to the gospel."

(Technically, in a modern academic sense, Cone would be considered the originator of Black Theology. But this form of God-talk was birthed in the fields, families, congregations, social movements, and the Black churches that have not only defined the nature of Black theology, but have also give meaning to who the United States of America is as a whole. So without a doubt, Cone is an innovator, but it is critical to note that his work is the codification of a spiritual and social legacy that has been alive and growing for hundreds of years.)

He also wrote, "Black theology is concerned with the total person as well as with the social structure in which we find ourselves."

For the Black prophetic tradition, the gospel begins with the human heart, extends to the whole person, and is complete insofar as it speaks to any and all social structures that are inhibiting the freedom of humanity. And these same voices show us that there is a straight line through the Bible of God's desire for justice—from Exodus, to the prophets, to Jesus, to the early church, and to the ultimate vision of oneness in revelation.

The Jesus within this legacy preaches that the love of God and the liberation of the oppressed cannot be separated.

Second. Jesus' solidarity with the oppressed and identification with the marginalized.

What is the significance of Jesus's actual life? What does it reveal to us? What value does it carry and offer for our day to day lives?

Does it not possess any salvific power in and of itself like conventional theology leads us to believe? Is the incarnation merely an expression of the divinity of Jesus for the sake of rendering him an acceptable sacrifice on the cross for the atonement of humanity's sin?

Yes, this is ridiculous, but it is also the conventional view taught in conservative Bible Colleges and churches across the country.

Sure, Jesus says some interesting things about the poor (we don't really pay attention to), imagines a radical lifestyle on the Sermon on the Mount (we don't really follow), and consistently includes and celebrates the outsider (in ways we're still uncomfortable with doing ourselves), but for so many the concrete life of Jesus is not actually essential for getting "saved" or becoming a Christian.

11

Is Jesus' life simply a prelude to the cross?

Was Jesus only "born to die" as one well known worship song proclaims?

The short answer is no.

The longer answer highlights how the minimization of the social substance of Jesus' status quo challenging and empire confronting ministry is what has drained Jesus' life of its transformative power and allowed the abstract white Jesus to remain so dominant. And as a result, has actually stripped our faith of its real power in society.

That was part of the long answer.

More on that later. But for now.

Kelly Brown Douglas.

While multiple facets of her work have shaped me, Douglas' clarity about how solidarity with the oppressed and identification with the marginalized are the defining dynamics of Jesus' earthly ministry are central to how I still see the way of Jesus today.

Brown Douglas writes,

"Jesus' ministry was disruptive of the social-political status quo...by associating with those who were socially marginalized."

Also,

"...an interpretation of Christianity that focuses on God's coming from heaven and becoming incarnate in Jesus, while sacrificing Jesus' ministry, unleashes the possibility for the emergence of the White Christ."

Jesus' earthly ministry to and identification with the poor and oppressed in his own first-century Palestinian context reveals a God who is unequivocally on the side of all who have been violently pushed into these marginal spaces. She also exposes how believing in Jesus without taking his concrete life seriously opens up a space for the abstract white Jesus to remain in power in our imaginations and our churches.

So Jesus's place in and empowerment of the edges is central to following him today.

Third. Uplifting hearts and tearing down broken systems.

The prophetic Black Christian tradition calls out not from the wilderness of the Ancient Near East, but from the inequality within the streets of the United States of America. It is not Isaiah, Jeremiah, Amos, and Micah naming the compromise, injustice, or participation in Babylon by the Jewish people, it is Sojourner, Fannie, Martin, and Cornel challenging the uncritical acceptance of the status quo by the church in the U.S. today.

Which is why the great writer and professor Derrick Bell wrote, "...we're a race of Jeremiahs, prophets calling the nation to repent."

These voices I named—along with all the other prophetic Black voices historically—have been fighting, speaking, organizing, preaching and calling the church into a more radical Jesus, and more just future. And each one is trying to help us see that "The gospel, then, is not a message about the salvation of individuals from the world, but news about a world transfigured right down to its basic structures."

Not just broken hearts but broken systems.

Not just love but liberation.

Not just turning your life over to God but over turning any institution that gets in the way of the life of God.

Without this liberating vision through Jesus that has something to say about injustice in any social form, we are left with that same abstract Jesus that allows whiteness and systemic evil to remain unchecked and in place.

And without the Concrete Jesus beautifully offered to all through the Black prophetic tradition, we are left with a faith that justified slavery, remained silent during lynchings, celebrated a "great awakening" of salvation while Black people remained in chains, resisted the Civil Rights Movement, and remains terrified of the idea that "Black Lives Matter" today.

We need a more concrete and liberating Jesus.

TWO

The Cosmic Christ

As a Christian, there are these funny moments where I feel uncomfortable when people use the name Jesus. I mean, how many pastors have you met who feel weird sometimes when people talk about Jesus?

For clarity, it's not that I have any problems with Jesus (I've actually given my entire life to his path), but I do have problems with where, how, and why some people use his name.

In these instances, if people said God, Spirit, or something similar, I'd be okay. But Jesus? When this happens, something within me responds, "I don't know about that."

"Jesus, I just want to say thank you for today..."

Hmmmm. Okay. So Jesus gave you this day? Jesus? Of Nazareth? The historical person Jesus who lived in the Ancient Near East in the 1st Century is also responsible for today happening? In Genesis 1 (which yes, I know is a poem), do you imagine it was a thirty year old Jesus who said, "let there be light?" If someone is thanking God or Spirit or Creator for the day? Definitely. But Jesus himself? That's an interesting concept.

"Jesus is always with you. Turn to Jesus and he can handle all of your problems right now."

Jesus is always with us? How does that work exactly? God being with us as His continuous Presence? Yes. Love always being available to us? Of course. The Eternal Christ who holds all things together holding us each time we surrender? Absolutely. But Jesus being with us right now? And how exactly do we turn to Jesus? Do we speak with him directly as if he is still a human being? Do we simply imagine a 33 year old Jesus and then have a conversation? "So Jesus, can you believe what Sheila said to me at work today!?" Christ being ever present as The Presence that sustains all of life? Yes. But handing our problems to Jesus? Not sure how that works.

"You know, I just need to get away and really be with Jesus you know?"

That's an interesting idea. A little getaway with Jesus of Nazareth. What exactly does that mean? Are you spending time with the same translucent Jesus we see helping Ronald Reagan sign the constitution in those hilarious memes? Do you just talk to Jesus as if he is still a human being in the way you are? Someone being intentionally present to God? Yes. Consciously experiencing your true self in Christ? Yes. Awareness of and awakening in Spirit? Yes. But spending time with Jesus? Hmmm...I am not sure about that.

"In this group of people, I saw Jesus here today."

So at a conference, through the diversity and conversations that were taking place, you saw Jesus? Jesus Christ? Mary and Joseph's son? The carpenter? You recognized Jesus here? Interesting. Seeing God manifest through diversity? Wonderful. You see the whole of Christ revealed in, through, and as the stories of the people? Beautiful. You see the Unity of Spirit within the parts of the individuals present? Yes. But what does it mean that you saw Jesus in and through a group of people? I don't fully get that.

Or let's think about moments of deep connection, powerful experience, or when we stumble upon beauty and awe.

We silently sit in the face of a sunset, and allow the motion of its color and the voice of its light to remind us once again, that somehow everything is okay.

Transcendence and beauty? Of course. Being present to the presence of God? Yes. Waking up to the sacredness of ever present Awareness? Absolutely. But would it be right for someone to say that was Jesus? Sacred? Of course. But Jesus? In the sunset? Like how some people see his face in a piece of toast? What does that mean exactly if someone were to say they experienced Jesus while watching a sunset?

We are in the middle of dinner with close friends, and through the smiles, laughter, food and wine, you suddenly realize that all of the goodness and mystery of life is present right here.

The fullness of life through your life? Yes. Gratitude and grace? Without a doubt. The full surrender to the eternal now? Sure. The substance of Christ? Definitely. But surely we wouldn't say we experienced Jesus in that moment would we? We could confidently say we felt the presence of God, but to say we felt Jesus? What does that mean if someone were to say that?

During a moment of silence, you experience a deep sense of union with God and unity with all of creation.

A sense of being seen and loved by God? Yes. The humbling experience of knowing you are simply a part of the entire fabric of the cosmos? Sure. The peace that comes from acceptance of and surrender to what is? Amazing. But would it makes sense for someone to walk back to their car after that experience and tell their friend that they spent time with Jesus?

I could keep going.

But let's stop for a second.

Do you see what I'm trying to speak to? Have you ever had questions like this? Have you ever heard someone say Jesus in a space that somehow seems like it doesn't fit? How many more could you come up with that would make the placement of Jesus in some people's conversations about the divine problematic?

For context.

Of course I understand what all of these people are attempting to speak of, but as a person who believes Jesus was fully human and fully divine, it still seems to me to be inappropriate or misguided to use the name Jesus instead of the words God or Christ at certain times.

And as a follower of Jesus, even though there are countless occasions, using the name Jesus to describe what is happening is misguided, I still believe there is a better way to speak of the divine spaciousness that transcends and includes everything.

And I do not believe I am the only one who thought this.

The Apostle Paul himself speaks of Jesus ascending in order to "fill the entire universe..." (Ephesians 4:10)

He writes about "the light of the knowledge of God's glory in the face of Jesus Christ." (2 Corinthians 4:6)

And even claims that, "He existed before all things, and all things are held together in him." (Colossians 1:17)

To add to those words, the writer of Hebrews says, "The Son is the light of God's glory and the imprint of God's being." (Hebrews 1:4)

These biblical writers speak of that which is...

Embedded within everything.

Filling the entire universe.

Existing before all things.

Holding all things together.

Paul is starting to reveal the mystery that was powerfully embodied in Jesus, yet existed before Jesus, and extends beyond Jesus. Here, Paul and the writer of Hebrews are articulating the power and presence of the Cosmic Christ.

Or even more simply, the Christ.

These visionary leaders in the early church were beginning to hint at and point to the Divine reality that has created, continues to animate, and binds together all of life since the inception of the universe itself—while also assuming that this force was inextricably linked with Jesus.

And this attempt to communicate this transcendent and concrete reality continues to this day.

Father Richard Rohr wrote, "Long before Jesus' personal incarnation, Christ was deeply embedded in all things—as all things!"

Paul Smith wrote, "The Cosmic Christ beyond Jesus is the transpersonal creative loving Face of God that creates all things and I whom all things hold together."

Karl Rahner wrote about, "the self-communication of God in the depths of existence—which we call grace, and in history—which we call Christ."

The infinite embedded within the finite, and the finite always existing within the infinite.

The universal presence that is born within, remains beyond, and keeps all things bound.

Beginning in the very beginning with the Big Bang, through atoms, molecules, cells, simple organisms, to human beings, and to cultural creation and the formation of communities, there has been a hidden evolutionary force at work driving this sacred process. From the depths of human creativity, through the unfolding of culture, within the organization of social bodies, to the expanding universe, and behind the curtain of the cosmic drama playing out as life itself, there is something good and powerful intentionally working.

This is the Cosmic Christ.

The Cosmic Christ has been unfolding in, through, and as the universe since the very beginning.

The Creative Drive of evolution itself.

The Organizing Principle within all forms of complexity.

The Transcendent Power immanent within the unity of life itself.

If any of this sounds a bit eclectic or unorthodox, remember that Paul claimed that Jesus ascended in order to "fill the entire universe" and that "He existed before all things, and all things are held together in him." Paul was deeply committed to the way of Jesus and beginning to imagine the shape of the cosmic reality of Christ.

And not only do these pioneering voices for humanity collectively name the Christ as the depth and drive of the universe, they also audaciously claim that this Presence was somehow fully present as Jesus.

To deepen this introduction to the Cosmic Christ, here are a few framing thoughts on the relationship between the Cosmic Christ and how it relates to the historical Jesus.

Jesus is the path that I follow, but Christ is the power that I surrender to.

Jesus is the incarnation of God in one place, Christ is the incarnation of God in all of time and space.

Jesus is concrete and historical, Christ is cosmic and eternal.

Jesus is when the flow took on form, when the substance became structure, and when the universal power became a specific person. Or, as Michael Dowd puts is, "Jesus is reality with a personality."

Christ is the ground, Jesus is the guide.

Christ is the terrain of everything, Jesus is the map.

Christ is the fullness of God, Jesus is the face of God.

Christ is that which holds all things together, draws humanity forward, fills everything, and remains the universal drive that guides our own individual evolution and the evolution of the universe itself.

Christ is also the embrace of a mother, the affirmation of a father, the fidelity of a lover, the grounding experience of eternal friendship, cosmic welcome, and the primal hospitality that welcomes us home through out first breath.

You can see why the medieval mystic, Mechthild of Magdeburg said, "The day of my spiritual awakening was the day I saw and knew I saw all things in God and God in all things."

The first chapter of the gospel of John is a beautiful and poetic opening about creation, eternity and the power of light that draws us into this dazzling tension between the cosmic nature of Christ and the concrete reality of Jesus. When the writer transitions between eternity and embodiment, he writes,

"The Word became flesh and made his dwelling among us. We have seen his glory, the glory of the one and only Son, who came from the Father, full of grace and truth" (John 1:14).

The word became flesh.

We are familiar with this passage and it speaks to the heart of the incarnation. And as the writer illuminates this idea even more, he adds, "No one has ever seen God, but the one and only Son, who is himself God and is in closest relationship with the Father, has made him known" (John 1:18).

So what does Jesus do?

He makes the Father known.

Other translations say

"He has shown us what God is like."

"He has revealed God to us."

"He has explained him"

In John 1:18, the English phrase "made him known" is actually the Greek word exēgēsato. And this specific version of this word is connected to the word eksēgéomai. And to eksēgéomai, meant to

bring forth,

explain,

narrate,

and or even to unfold.

And this Greek word exēgēsato is where we get our English word exegesis from. And people who have studied biblical interpretation know that the process of exegesis involves the interpretation or explaining of the meaning of a particular passage of Scripture. Here, John is revealing something powerful.

The embodiment of Jesus is the explanation of God.

Jesus reveals who God is and what God is like.

We could even say that God is unfolding in and through Jesus.

So if Cornel West says that justice is what love looks like in public, John is saying that Jesus is what God looks like in public.

If Christ is the presence, Jesus is the path. The cosmic energy of the Christ is concretely expressed in and as Jesus. The universal truth of everything is embodied in the particular life of one person.

Or, we could say God is what Jesus does.

Christ is the open field of everything, and Jesus is the way through this field helping give us access to all that is.

The indivisible nexus between the Cosmic Christ and the Concrete Jesus communicates an infinite relationship that keeps us moving back and forth between the universal and the particular, eternity and embodiment, and awareness and action.

We need the great activists, leaders, and writers from the Black prophetic tradition to continue to call us back to a life committed to justice, compassion, and incarnation through the liberating Jesus. We also need the mystics to help awaken us to universal drive of evolution, the bonding cosmic energy of Spirit, and the universally affirming Presence of God through the reality of the Cosmic Christ.

We need both.

Without the liberating Jesus,

we are unable to see the humanity of all people.

We are left with an individualistic gospel that is not thick enough, complex enough, and powerful enough to confront systemic forms of injustice.

While referring to the limitations of believing in Jesus without this larger vision of the Cosmic Christ, Richard Rohr wrote, "Jesus can hold together one group or religion. Christ can hold together everything."

Without the Cosmic Christ,

our faith too easily remains tribal, ethnocentric, and antagonistic to those we see on the outside.

It remains embarrassingly difficult to provide a coherent cosmology and to make sense of the sacred history of the universe.

Unconditional love becomes virtually impossible to access for ourselves or to be comfortable allowing for others who are different than us.

The cosmic Christ liberates us to rest in that wide open space of Spirit and know for ourselves that we are loved by Christ and safe in Christ.

THREE

Love and Liberation

Love

One of the most famous passages written about love comes from the Apostle Paul in 1 Corinthians 13. If you have ever been to a wedding, you may have heard it before.

Paul wrote, "Love is patient, love is kind. It does not envy, it does not boast, it is not proud. It does not dishonor others, it is not self-seeking, it is not easily angered, it keeps no record of wrongs. Love does not delight in evil but rejoices with the truth. It always protects, always trusts, always hopes, always perseveres." (1 Corinthians 13:4-7)

He also dares to suggest that "Love never fails." (v.8)

Powerful stuff.

But what is usually not mentioned during these ceremonies are the first three verses of this chapter. Paul begins this beautiful and poetic section with these three statements:

"If I speak in the tongues of men or of angels, but do not have love, I am only a resounding gong or a clanging cymbal." (v.1)

"If I have the gift of prophecy and can fathom all mysteries and all knowledge, and if I have a faith that can move mountains, but do not have love, I am nothing." (v. 2)

"If I give all I possess to the poor and give over my body to hardship that I may boast, but do not have love, I gain nothing." (v. 3)

Paul sees that religious or moral actions without love is noise and nothingness.

What else do you think we can add to Paul's list today?

If I can articulate orthodox beliefs in confessional Christianity, but do not know love, it means nothing.

If I use the name of Jesus incessantly, but am unwilling to extend the universal love of God to all people, I am nothing.

Or if I believe in Jesus but have not been personally transformed by love, I am merely an empty container.

Love.

The ground is love.

The goal is love.

Love truly is the "deepest structure of the universe" as the anthropologist and Jesuit mystic Pierre De Chardin claimed.

And let's remember, before Paul, Jesus provocatively defined this conversation about love.

"Hearing that Jesus had silenced the Sadducees, the Pharisees got together. One of them, an expert in the law, tested him with this question: "Teacher, which is the greatest commandment in the Law?"

Jesus replied: "'Love the Lord your God with all your heart and with all your soul and with all your mind.' This is the first and greatest commandment. And the second is like it: 'Love your neighbor as yourself.' All the Law and the Prophets hang on these two commandments." (Matthew 27:34-40)

Jesus' answer is love.

Here's what I think.

Religious leaders want to believe this, but their precious beliefs get in the way. No matter how passionately clergy preach about unconditional love, eventually they must return...

To their beliefs.

To their doctrines.

To their dogma.

Without even realizing it, they once again start slicing love into pieces (as if it can be sliced), and allowing their precious beliefs to parcel out these pathetic fragments up amongst all of the various sojourners based on race, creed, sexuality, or whatever their preferred dividing markers are. They attempt to divide that which is indivisible, withhold that which cannot be held back, and provide rations to others without noticing they are minimizing their own portion at the cosmic feast table of love in the process.

Jesus insists this is about love.

Paul claims that without it, we are nothing.

One gospel writer even dared to claim that God is love.

And yet we keep allowing systems to tame her, beliefs and boundaries to micromanage her, and untransformed religious leaders to dare to try and control her.

After getting married in Hawai'i at twenty-two years old, my wife and I moved into our first apartment together in Costa Mesa, CA. Those early years of marriage we were both still in school, working in restaurants, and making things happen for ourselves. It was a beautiful time in our lives.

As I shared in my previous book, our apartment had this fireplace that would turn on by the simple winding of a knob (yes, that was the story where I was praying naked in front of the fire).

I used to spend a significant amount of time sitting in silence and listening to sermons being preached by the warmth of the blaze. Receiving wisdom from the color and movement of the flames. And responding to the invitation of the Spirit through the heat of the roaring fire.

(Okay, the knob didn't quite make a roaring fire in that small apartment, but it sounds better.)

And one night, as I was meditating in front of the fire, it just hit me out of nowhere.

Not just conceptually, but experientially. Not just in my understanding, but in the direct realization within my own body, which is the only way transformation actually works.

Do you know what this realization was?

Love just is.

Love.

Just.

Is.

And this seemingly non-revolutionary/revolutionary idea demanded that I write something down immediately. And here's exactly what I wrote in that moment about sixteen years ago.

Love is immanent and yet transcendent
We experience love but we never contain love
We do not own love
Love is a reality that just is
Love exists whether we are a part of her or not
Love is an absolute mystery
Love naturally gives herself
Love is not an it
Love is not a thing
Love is not an object
Love is bigger than our experience of her
Any time we decide to withhold love from another it is not love
we are withholding,
as if love is something we possess and contain within ourselves,
it is merely ourselves we are withholding
Love just is...
Love is a mystery to be participated in
If we allow her
If we trust her
If we let go
She will transform us

The imagery that came with this energetic and embodied realization was that love is like a mist that is moving toward and giving herself to all people at all times equally. We may not be aware of it or believe in it, but love is infinitely present and inviting us to wake up and know for ourselves.

The Cosmic Christ reveals itself as the universal affirmation of matter and unconditional love for humanity.

Love has no doctrines,

Love does not participate in conversations about orthodoxy, and damn sure does not build courtrooms to judge cases of heresy.

Love is not involved in any division, discrimination, or separation.

Love just is.

This realization was not a revelation that was unique to me, I simply joined the myriad eyes that have been recognized by this love for ages.

Around five thousand years ago, Moses heard the voice of God pass in front of him saying, "The Lord, the Lord, the compassionate and gracious God, slow to anger, abounding in love and faithfulness..." (Exodus 34:6)

When King David was teaching some of his people to praise God, one the phrases he gave to them to do so was "Give thanks to the Lord, for he is good; his love endures forever." (1 Chronicles 16:34)

When the Psalmist was inviting the collective imagination to remember God, he declared, "Remember, Lord, your compassion and your faithful love, for they have existed from antiquity." (Psalm 25: 6)

The Cosmic Christ has been unfolding through love in the universe in a million different places, and as humanity through a million different faces.

Do we think God was waiting for billions of years since the inception of the universe to allow the love of Christ to be fully present in this world? Has God been withholding love from creation until the day Jesus was born?

Well, no.

When Jesus prayed to God for his friends in John 17, he hoped that they would see his glory because, "the glory you have given me because you loved me before the creation of the world." (John 17:24)

When Paul wrote to the Corinthians, he told them that, "love never ends." (1 Corinthians 13:8)

The love Jesus referred to not only pre-dated his birth and life, but was a living reality before creation itself and Paul described love as a presence or flow that never ends. So this love seems to have no beginning, no end, and is an indivisible and inclusive embrace that is linked together by God, Christ, and Jesus.

The Cosmic Christ is how we name the eternally creative and universally accessible reality that is born again and again through out the life of the universe and within the diverse journey of humanity.

Which is why we should never be surprised when we see the energetic signature of Christ's love written on the lives of and present in the words of great spiritual thinkers from any and all traditions.

The Buddhist monk Thich Nhat Hanh wrote, "To love is to recognize; to be loved is to be recognized by the other."

The inter-spiritual teacher Mirabai Starr claimed that, "It lasts, and will last forever, because God loves it. Everything that is has its being through the love of God."

And the Sufi 2th Century Muslim mystic IBN Arabi said, "I follow the religion of love: whatever way Love's camel takes, that is my religion and faith."

The love of Christ can never be contained by the religion who bears the name of Jesus. Instead it transcends and includes the Christian tradition within its cosmic embrace of all things, all cultures, all traditions, and all people.

Love is not a thing, it is that which holds together everything. Love is not simply something you do, it is what the universe actually is at the deepest layer. Love is not just one thing we receive from God, it is the very substance of God that embraces and sustains all things.

The Cosmic Christ's presence has been flowing in and through creation from the beginning, and those who are most in tune with its frequency have continued to recognize its true identity as love.

Which is why we can never separate the words of Jesus when he claimed, "God is love," and the words of the poet Rumi who recognized that, "Love is the bridge between you and everything."

Liberation

I remember sitting down at a bar in Orange County, CA and having a beer with an older pastor. I was around twenty-seven years old and getting ready to move back to Hawai'i to start a new church. This pastor who had given his life to the church and was interested in guiding me on my path of pastoring, was substantially different than I was, and I wasn't sure he was fully aware of that.

He was more conservative theologically and carried a drastically divergent imagination for what the future of the church should like. I remember at one point in the conversation saying to him,

"You know, I'm more occupy Wall Street than I am Wall Street. And I am more MLK than I am Billy Graham."

I was trying to help him understand the distinctions between us that I felt would make it difficult to keep building the kind of relationship that would allow him to speak into the life of the church I was getting ready to build. And also to help him see that he may in fact, be uncomfortable with who I was and where I was going.

More Dr. Martin Luther King Jr. than Billy Graham.

Let's clarify this statement a little bit.

In 1976, the reverend Jesse Jackson shared some provocative thoughts about the differences between Martin Luther King Jr. and Billy Graham in an interview he did for Christianity Today. One of the key statements he made while referring to the Israelites being enslaved in Egypt was,

"...that Billy Graham would have preached to the slaves in Egypt and converted their souls and told them to go back to the fields; then he'd have gone and played golf with Pharaoh..."

(Which is hilarious by the way.)

Then he said, "Dr. King would have preached to change their souls and then taken them to Canaan."

For Graham, salvation was individualistic and strictly about saving souls. For King, the gospel included our personal life with God, but was also about justice and its interconnected link with social and economic liberation. Jackson saw the problems with the individualistic gospel of white evangelicalism and also the possibility of liberation leading to a more whole gospel in the preaching and life of Dr. King—and radically in the concrete life of Jesus.

Without including liberation in the gospel, we are always left with a truncated Jesus.

A Jesus who cares about saving our souls but not valuing our bodies.

A Jesus who sees people individually, but does not have a vision for justice collectively.

A Jesus who has the power to get us into heaven in the afterlife, but is impotent while BIPOC and LGBTQ+ people are catching hell in this life, and in our country.

Preaching a gospel that does not make room for liberation in its heart is what helped pave the path for the absurdity of the white Christian nationalism that is so prevalent today. It empowers people to uphold and reinforce the unjust social status quo and creates entire communities of indifference.

When referring to the lived reality of the abstract Jesus in the United States, or as she calls it, the white christ, Kelly Brown Douglas wrote, "American Christians are too busy saving the souls of white Christians from burning in hell-fire to save the lives of black ones from present burning in fires kindled by white Christians."

Why would Christians waste their time with injustice and liberating actual bodies when God has called us to preach the gospel, right? Why would we give our lives to fight for the liberation of the oppressed when the real liberation is found for our souls in heaven? Why would we work to overturn and overcome dehumanizing systems when our real enemy is personal sin?

This is how an overwhelming amount of Christians think, right?

But here's the problem.

The abstract white Jesus focused on saving us from hell renders us almost completely indifferent to the systemic evil causing the suffering of people today.

Sure. People might feel bad sometimes, but they aren't really following Jesus in a way that causes them to dismantle the structures that are suffocating those who have been forced to the margins.

Perhaps the fruit of the abstract and white Jesus of the individualistic gospel is what helped lead the writer Danté Stewart, in his epistle to America, "Shoutin' In The Fire" to write,

"It wasn't Jesus nor James Baldwin who radicalized me.

It was white people.

Apathetic white people."

A Jesus without liberation always disciples people into apathy in the face of injustice.

In 2010, during my first year at Fuller Theological Seminary, I took an Intro to Black Theology class taught by the great Dr. Ralph C. Watkins, that changed my life forever. Every single three hour lecture was a spell binding

journey that would widen my understanding of Jesus, deepen my apprehension of the gospel, and help me fall further in love with the Black prophetic tradition in the United States.

This is where I would be introduced to Black and Womanist writers and thinkers like James Cone, Kelly Brown Douglas, Renita Weems, Katie Canon, Jaquelyn Grant, Dwight Hopkins, Will Coleman, and Cornel West to name a few.

And this experience is where I would hear the stories of great Black liberators, leaders, and activists like Sojourner Truth, Ida B. Wells, and one of the greatest Christians of the 20th Century, Fannie Lou Hamer.

From the unmatched presence of my professor Dr. Watkins, to the imaginations of some of the greatest Black and Womanist theologians, to the grounded work for freedom by these great leaders, they all shared a collective heart for one thing when it came to Jesus.

Liberation.

These incredible voices and diverse legacies together created an atmosphere that made it impossible to not see.

There is no gospel without liberation

There is no truth without liberation.

There is no real Jesus without liberation.

Cone wrote, "...because the God of black experience was not a metaphysical idea. God was the God of history, the Liberator of the oppressed from bondage. Jesus was not an abstract Word of God, but God's Word made flesh who came to set the prisoner free."

It is the clarity of this tradition that offers the gift of the Concrete Jesus who calls us to liberation. This liberating Jesus exposes the danger of the abstract Jesus who does not seem to even care about the real need for liberation and remains unable to see the full humanity of the people in need of liberation.

This symphony of Black voices call us back to Exodus—the defining moment for the Israelites in the Old Testament. And one after another, dare us to see this moment of liberation for exactly what it is—a personal, social, economic, and political liberation of God's people from an oppressive empire.

So when Cornel West says, "For prophetic Christianity, the two inseparable notions of freedom are existential freedom and social freedom," the engine for this movement toward freedom began in that Exodus movement toward liberation.

There is a straight line though from the liberation in Exodus, to the Prophets challenging the injustice of multiple empires, to Jesus' liberating words and solidarity with oppressed, to the ultimate poetic vision of justice in Revelation 21, demonstrating that personal salvation and social liberation are at the center of the Spirit's work in this world.

In the same way, there is a straight line through the Bible showing the God of liberation who aligns himself with those on the underside of power. There is also a straight line through the history of the U.S. for a strong majority of white churches who refuse to see the need for liberation, and who choose to align themselves with toxic forms of power too.

From Slavery, to silence during lynchings, to the Great Awakening preachers holding slaves, to not supporting civil rights, to the current normalization of Black brutality and murder by the police, we see what happens when churches and a country do not carry on the legacy of the concrete and liberating Jesus.

So, when Cole Arthur Riley claims, "This is a world that demonizes those who will transgress the system but has a great sympathy for the system itself[,]" maybe this is the world that is naturally created when we preach the individualistic, abstract, and white Jesus.

Do you know what Jesus said in his first sermon?

He stood up in a synagogue, drew upon the prophet Isaiah, and astonishingly declared,

> "The Spirit of the Lord is on me,
> because he has anointed me
> to proclaim good news to the poor.
>
> He has sent me to proclaim freedom for the prisoners
> and recovery of sight for the blind, to set the oppressed free,
> to proclaim the year of the Lord's favor." (Luke 4:18-19)

Centering the poor.

Freedom for the imprisoned.

Liberation of the oppressed.

The audacity of Jesus to begin his public ministry with these words. This is the sharp edge of truth that effortlessly cuts through unjust systems of power and the collective ideology that upholds them. This proclamation is a jarring word that carries the power to unhinge people from their addictive reliance on worldly power and their hidden favoritism toward the rich. This moment established a way of being that is not focused on comforting individuals who benefit from an oppressive system, but rather has at its starting point the liberation of those have been oppressed by the system.

This socially radical and liberation oriented sermon could not be preached in the majority of churches in the United States of America today.

And to be honest, it never would be.

So what do most churches do? What do most pastors say? That these words are somehow about private or personal matters. They take this radical social vision of Jesus and drain it of all of its liberative power, and misrepresent it as merely spiritual ideas for the individual soul.

Churches who have been formed by the abstract white Jesus do not see liberation in this sermon. They cannot see the centrality of compassion to the impoverished. And because of the abstract Jesus they follow, they are almost completely unable to embrace the way of Jesus as a freedom movement for those who have been imprisoned by the state.

Commitment to the abstract white Jesus requires us to deradicalize the social power of Jesus' message through spiritualizing these words into piety for the individual.

The good news is for those who are poor in spirit.

The prisoners who need freedom are individuals who are enslaved to sin.

The oppression we are freed from are the "spiritual" forces that holds us back individually and internally.

The abstract Jesus fails to see the urgent need for concrete liberation for the oppressed in his time, and thus forms churches who fail the real needs for oppressed and marginalized people in our time. The conventional white Jesus that carries the most power in our culture has virtually nothing to say to the most obvious forms of injustice, and thus has no role in the collective movement toward liberation.

But in this sermon, Jesus actually told us what the heart of his message was. And in the Concrete Jesus we see in the gospels, the heart of liberation is everywhere.

Thirty years before Jesus preached this message telling us who he was and what he was about, his mother Mary preached another message telling us who he would be and what he would be about.

And what did she say Jesus was going to do?

Scatter the proud.

Bring down rulers from their thrones.

Fill the hungry with good things.

Send the rich away empty.

It is right there in the first chapter of the gospel of Luke. Mary, the blessed mother of Jesus declares that her son's role as king is good news for the poor and a legitimate social and political threat to the rich and powerful.

Jesus and Mary both explicitly told us about the liberating nature of the gospel.

And then for the duration of the gospels, we witness a Jesus that declares the poor as blessed, says it's virtually impossible for rich people to enter the kingdom of heaven, elevates the role of peacemakers, calls religious leaders hypocrites for their capitulation to the Roman state, identifies with the marginalized, confronts and challenges the entire oppressive economic system by flipping tables, and is eventually crucified as an enemy of the state.

Jesus told us he was going to center the poor and liberation, and then he embodied this message his entire public life.

But privilege, power, and the abstract white Jesus do not allow us to see this, which the great James Cone told us was happening about forty years ago when he said,

"Because most biblical scholars are the descendants of the advantaged class, it is to be expected that they would minimize Jesus gospel of liberation for the poor by interpreting poverty as a spiritual condition unrelated to social and political phenomena."

May the liberating Jesus from the Black prophetic tradition and the gospels give us the eyes to see the foundation of liberation that has been right there all along.

FOUR

Our Body and The Body of Christ

Our Body

We have a hard time feeling at home in our bodies.

Isn't that strange?

The only vehicle we have for our participation in the unfolding of the Divine life itself can be experienced as inhospitable.

Clunky.

Awkward.

Uncomfortable.

At times we can even feel unwelcome in our own bodies—and somehow it feels like we are both the one who is doing the unwelcoming and the one receiving the lack of welcome.

We can subtly view our body as a problem.

Or an obstacle.

Or an embarrassment.

In her research on shame, Brené Brown discovered that the number one issue related to the shame women experience was connected to their relationship with their bodies. There is a multi-billion dollar a year plastic surgery industry focused on transforming how we look. And we are bombarded with advertisements telling us all the ways we are lacking fullness and beauty as our bodies.

Men are not exempt from this either. According to data from the Aesthetic Society and the American Society of Plastic Surgeons, cosmetic surgery for men has also been on the rise the past few years as well.

We seem to be immersed in a popular cultural imagination that makes it seemingly impossible for people to age gracefully. A culture that makes it difficult to age peacefully is connected to a larger relational ecosystem where it is challenging to feel at home in our bodies.

One of the weird things about getting older is witnessing the people you grew up watching on television completely alter their faces through an attempt to appear younger and more desirable or hirable. Sometimes I have this voice from deep within offering a hope or prayer for people as they age, "It's okay to get old."

I could go on about the breadth and complexity of ways we feel that we are at war with our bodies, but we all know this struggle is very real and present in and around us.

Which is why I will say it again: we have a hard time feeling at home in our bodies.

And yet, the great rabbi Abraham Joshua Heschel said, "How embarrassing for humans to be the greatest miracle on earth and not understand it."

The greatest miracle on earth.

Or as the creation poem in Genesis 1 said, "very good."

Not despite our bodies,

but inside our bodies,

and through our bodies,

and especially, as our bodies.

Being connected with God should lead us to being at peace in our bodies.

We are not simply spiritual beings seeking redemption for our souls, we are human beings longing to feel welcomed with the entirety of our existence. Salvation does not feel like relief from escaping hell, it feels like sitting down on a couch and being loved so deeply we are finally convinced that we are home.

Our body comfortable.

Our mind at peace.

Our Spirit safe.

The creation story in Genesis 1 is an invitation for humanity to trust that we're home. To believe the most foundational act of God is one of hospitality. To dare to trust that salvation means we are welcome here.

The world is good.

We are good.

And we have a sacred task to care for our home.

I promise. It's all right there "In the beginning."

So when Arthur Cole Riley says, "I want a faith that loves the whole of me" I believe she is articulating a universal prayer *of* humanity, and a cosmic truth *for* humanity. We do have a faith that loves and affirms the whole of us from the very beginning.

And the Christ is calling us back to the simplicity and sacredness of being fully ourselves.

In John 1:14, the gospel writer dares to claim that "The Word became flesh and made his dwelling among us."

The Word.

That which was "with God and was God." (v.1)

Through whom "all things were made." (v.3)

The "light of all mankind." (v.4)

The "true light that gives light to everyone." (v.9)

The one the "world was made through." (v.10)

Oh.

That Word?

This eternally present, creative, and universally enlightening Word became flesh in Jesus?

So the human body became the ultimate medium for the life of God to be expressed. Flesh and blood became the place where Spirit was the most visible in creation. This organic mix of blood, hair, skin, glands, tissue, muscles, joints, and bones is the space that the creative source has chosen to reveal Himself to the world?

When the Word became flesh,

the Universal became personal.

the Cosmic became concrete.

and the Eternal Christ was born out of and into this world as the Historical Jesus.

(I know passionate preachers around Christmas like to say things like, "God stepped down into human history," but if the Eternal Word has always been present in creation, that doesn't actually make sense.)

So much of historical Christian teaching created an artificial divide and antagonism between the spiritual and the material, between spirit and body, and between the soul and flesh. And this dualistic way of seeing is precisely what Jesus came to reveal as a lie in the incarnation.

This dualistic lie of flesh and Spirit being at odds has been woven into the cultural fabric of the West, and fortified at the center of so much of the ice of the church. Think about all of the sermons that made you internalize that flesh and our bodies are somehow inherently sinful or evil. Or consider the horrific concept of total depravity that made it virtually impossible to hear the sound of your own voice and know your own desires from within.

But Genesis 1 offers us an alternative imagination that transcends this dualistic vision and invites us to experience real unity within the sacred site of our own lives.

The Spirit as material.

The Spirit as flesh.

And the Spirit as body.

While the profound truth of Incarnation carries a surplus of meaning for our lives, there is one thing it means for sure.

The Incarnation is the divine affirmation of the goodness of the human body.

In this poetic creation story in John 1—which is one of the defining stories for the entire Bible—there is no shame or tension for the writer about Spirit and flesh being woven together. Genesis 1 reveals that matter and Spirit have never been separate, and John re-affirms that union in the person of Jesus.

The living mystic Cynthia Bourgeault, when referring to the incarnation, spoke of God being, "fully at home within the conditions of finitude. So that form itself poses no impediment to divinity." Jesus' body did not get in the way of the divine, it became the clearest way for the divine.

Jesus' body was the ultimate medium for Spirit.

And so is yours.

Your body is an integral part of the good that God declares you are and Spirit is poetically entangled with your skin.

Your body is not something to be tolerated by you, it is something that is celebrated by God.

You are the greatest miracle, and right now, there is no fully embodied and present you without your body. No matter how you feel about it, this is the most profound medium for God. If the medium is the message, then your awake, alive, and engaged body moving towards others in love is somehow the apex of not only what it means to be human, but of life itself.

Believing in the incarnation of Jesus means nothing if you don't trust in your own.

Trusting the incarnation and the sacredness of our bodies empowers us to resist any forces, whether political or personal, that attempt to degrade or devalue our bodies.

One day I was sitting in that same Intro to Black Theology class and my professor Dr. Ralph C. Watkins was talking about James Brown.

(By the way, one of the many reasons I love Black Spirituality is how so many of its greatest teachers seamlessly flow with such an intertextual social and theological imagination. In one lecture, Doc Watkins could go from Jay-Z to Jesus, from the Blues to liberation theology, and from the oppressive empires of Israel's past to exactly what is happening in our own political context of oppression today.)

And as he was taking us on a journey, he talked about the power of hearing James Brown emphatically sing, "Say it loud. I'm Black and I'm proud." This song was first heard on the radio in the year 1968. I will never forget how Dr. Watkins reflected on the power of that statement by suggesting that some Black people at that time may have never heard that declaration publicly in their life before.

Black.

And proud.

Their Black body as a source of goodness. Their Blackness as beautiful. Not something to apologize for, but to be proud of.

In the face of historical, cultural, and institutionalized white supremacy that had leveraged all its power to get Black people to believe that their bodies were inherently evil and less than human—James brown singing "Say it loud. I'm Black and I'm proud" was an Incarnational moment.

That declaration was a refusal to accept any deformed definition that degraded the fullness of who he was as a Black man in America. Brown teaches us that the incarnation liberates us and demands that we affirm the fullness of who we are no matter what anybody else says or has been trying to say for hundreds of years.

Candice Benbow wrote, "But I knew it was in the doctrine of creation where I would situate the most important argument I'd ever make: if all of creation is holy, then Black girls and women are holy, too."

Jaquelyn Grant wrote, "womanist just means being and acting out of who you are…"

Which is also why it is so powerful when Bishop Yvette Flunder proclaims, "I am an avowed womanist and reconciling liberation theologian who dances in the Spirit and speaks in tongues."

And in a social context where Whiteness has been leveraged culturally, politically, and psychologically to diminish the sacredness of the lives of Black women, the Incarnational affirmation of their bodies is not only a courageous affirmation of their own bodies, but also a daring invitation for all of us to uphold the sacredness of our bodies.

These statements put on display how Spirit being at home in creation and the Incarnation of Jesus is what empowers us to feel at home in this universe and trust in the incarnation of our own existence.

The Body of Christ

"Christ has no body but yours."

The 16th Century Spanish mystic St. Teresa of Ávila proclaimed this powerful truth in the 16th Century.

She said Christ has no body but yours.

Which now means Christ has no body but ours.

Interesting.

Is she saying that Christ always expresses itself through flesh and blood?

Is she saying that our lives in alignment with the life of Christ become the very site for divine revelation and presence in the exact same way that Jesus' was?

And is the you implied in yours us as individuals? The harmony of our collective evolutionary movement to the future? Is the you implied in yours the Church? Is it everyone? Is it all people in the beauty of our diversity caring for and committed to the health of this planet and the wholeness of humanity?

Yes.

I believe that is exactly what she meant and that she was talking about all people.

One of the most profound implications of this statement about being the body of Christ is the life altering idea that God does not just show up through us,

but as us.

As us.

This revolutionary proposal does not only go back to Teresa of Ávila in the 16th Century, it goes all the way back to The Apostle Paul in the First Century. Think about all of the space Paul gave to this idea.

"Now you are Christ's body, and individually members of it..." (1 Corinthians 12:27)

"For just as we have many members in one body and all the members do not have the same function, so we, who are many, are one body in Christ, and individually members one of another." (Romans 12:4-5)

"For even as the body is one and yet has many members, and all the members of the body, though they are many, are one body, so also is Christ." (1 Corinthians 12:12)

"There is one body and one Spirit..." Ephesians 4:4

"Now I rejoice in my sufferings for your sake, and in my flesh I do my share on behalf of His body, which is the church, in filling up what is lacking in Christ's afflictions." (Colossians 1:24)

"For by one Spirit we were all baptized into one body, whether Jews or Greeks, whether slaves or free, and we were all made to drink of one Spirit." (1 Corinthians 12:13)

"Is not the cup of blessing which we bless a sharing in the blood of Christ? Is not the bread which we break a sharing in the body of Christ? Since there is one bread, we who are many are one body; for we all partake of the one bread." (1 Corinthians 10:16-17)

"...but speaking the truth in love, we are to grow up in all aspects into Him who is the head, even Christ, from whom the whole body, being fitted and held together by what every joint supplies, according to the proper working of each individual part, causes the growth of the body for the building up of itself in love." (Ephesians 4:15-16)

"...so that there may be no division in the body, but that the members may have the same care for one another. And if one member suffers, all the members suffer with it; if one member is honored, all the members rejoice with it." (1 Corinthians 12:25-26)

"...for no one ever hated his own flesh, but nourishes and cherishes it, just as Christ also does the church, because we are members of His body. (Ephesians 5:29-30)

"Let the peace of Christ rule in your hearts, to which indeed you were called in one body..."(Col. 3:15)

This progressive, even avant-garde leader in the early church had this vision of the church as the body of Christ. Not just a carrier of the Spirit, but the body of Christ. Not merely loyal workers trying to be obedient to a God outside of us, but awakened members of the body of the ever present flow of Christ in this world.

Christ has no body but ours.

There have been many sacred moments where I have stood in a circle with others holding hands while centering ourselves and praying together. And in some of those moments I would inevitably end up saying something about the reality that God is not just present in the person next to you, but God is actually present as the person next to you.

If I were to walk in to a party you were hosting, and you introduced me to some of your friends, what would you say?

This is my friend Kevin present in this body? (Which would be weird.)

Or, meet Kevin as he flows through his body? (Which would be even weirder.)

Or would you just say this is Kevin, because you operate with the assumption that I am my body, so I am allowed to just show up as my body? (Which I know, still sounds weird, but I'm making a point.)

The invitation to become the body of Christ dares us to believe that the life of God is not just unfolding in this world through us or is present in us, but that Spirit is developing through this world as us.

As.

Us.

Which is why I think of the words from the remarkable wisdom teacher Barbara Holmes, "The Church is not called to be a model of corporate organization but rather an organic and responsive body of Christ."

Maybe it is true. Christ has not body but ours.

The March on Washington happened near the Lincoln Memorial on August 28th, 1963. While America was still attempting to live into its ideals of democracy, this march focused on jobs, freedom, and the ongoing movement toward equality and justice for Black people in a post-slavery and civil rights era.

And during the struggle for civil rights, Medgar Evers' assassination lead to outrage and became a catalyst for this march.

Some skeptics and resisters to the movement prepared for a riot, and even JFK stated that he believed the mass demonstration was ill-timed. Dr. Martin Luther King Jr., brilliantly responded by saying, "Frankly, I have never engaged in any direct-action movement which did not seem ill-timed."

While some people prepared for a nightmare, the rest of the people heard about a dream.

This demonstration in Washington D.C. was a stunning visual scene. 250,000 people marching and gathering together to make known the collective desire for a more just and equal America. In unity, the people were hearing about a dream for the future that looked and felt more like Jesus' vision of the Kingdom of God. Where all people live in oneness beyond the version of America that was essentially built for white men to rule.

What was that monumental moment like? How did it feel to be a part of that body of people?

The bodies moving in unison,

the tenacious and hopeful smiles on the faces of the elders,

the laughter of the kids, and the voices of dignity and resistance singing themselves into the future of God.

This was was a powerful collective embodiment and enactment of the evolutionary movement of the Christ in and through our world.

In an illuminating fashion, Cole Arthur Riley profoundly wrote, "Activism is the body of justice."

Perhaps that March on Washington is wired into the collective brain of America so deeply because of how powerfully it embodied Christ. If activism is the body of justice, and justice is a central part of Christ's desire for the planet, then those people acting together for the sake of the future were the body of Christ in that setting. The body of justice is at a broader level, the body of Christ showing up in her fullness for the sake of equitable future.

Maybe this is how it always works.

Being present during suffering is the body of compassion. Which is the body of Christ.

Aligning ourselves and our interests with the oppressed is the body of solidarity. Which is the body of Christ.

Using our energy for the sake of another's flourishing is the body of service. Which is the body of Christ.

We awaken to the Christ and become the body of Christ any time our lives individually or collectively are aligned with and are an extension of the way of Jesus in our world. To follow the Concrete Jesus through our world means we take seriously our calling to become the body of Christ for the world.

Which is exactly why there are countless moments that I can witness and say, "That is the body of Christ. Or simply, this is the Christ."

When a therapist holds a nonjudgmental and affirming space for another person to risk being deeply human, this is the body of Christ.

When your resources are centered around the flourishing of the most vulnerable, this is the body of Christ.

When a group of activists speak the truth and call out concrete forms of injustice and oppression, this is the body of Christ.

The Womanist scholar and writer Dr. Monica Coleman courageously tells her story in her book, "Bipolar Faith: A Black Woman's Journey With Depression and Faith." It is a mesmerizing journey that takes the reader through her experience at Harvard, being sexually assaulted, dealing with severe depression, going to Seminary, family history, and eventually moving to California.

The honesty of this book can both make you uncomfortable and empower you to own every part of your own story in the same way Dr. Coleman has.

And near the end, as she is sharing about how she continues to move forward and sustain a relationship with God and her own well being, she writes, "I rebuild with God in the same way: meal by meal, prayer by prayer, stitch by stitch, dance by dance, song by song."

I love that.

Meal by meal.

Prayer by prayer

Stitch by stitch.

Dance by dance.

Song by song.

Where is God in this journey of health and healing? How does Christ remain present and reveal itself? What does the body of Christ look and feel like in this person's experience?

The body of Christ sits down with her during these meals. The body of Christ prays with her, and maybe even lays hands on her during these prayers. The body of Christ picks up those tiny needles and stitches with her as she herself is being stitched back together. And the body of Christ dances and sings with her on her way to the future.

Remember that Teresa of Avilá quote I began this chapter with? "Christ has not body but yours." That line is actually a part of a larger prayer or poem that she wrote. And what she wrote in full is this:

"Christ has no body but yours,

No hands, no feet on earth but yours,

Yours are the eyes with which he looks compassion on this world,

Yours are the feet with which he walks to do good,

Yours are the hands, with which he blesses all the world.

Yours are the hands, yours are the feet,

Yours are the eyes, you are his body.

Christ has no body now but yours."

You are the body of Christ.

We are the Christ whenever we allow the Spirit to work in us, through us, and as us for the sake of the world.

FIVE

Calling Forward and Calling Out

Calling Forward

In the beginning, there was a bang.

And it was a big bang.

From atoms to molecules to cells to single cell organisms to human beings to tribes to a global sense of community, to ecosystems, to the biosphere, and to the interconnectedness of the universe as a whole, since the beginning, there has been growth, evolution, and movement.

The brain evolving from the reptilian structure, to the limbic system, to the complex neocortex.

Human beings way of seeing evolving from ethnocentric, to world-centric, to cosmo-centric.

Our sense of community evolving from ethno-tribes, to a common humanity, to an interconnected universe.

We are historically situated in a sacred history of billions of years of evolution beautifully taking place within an even larger unfolding and still expanding universe.

Growth.

Change.

Evolution.

When you consider the fine tuning of the universe and the ever increasing forms of complexity of life, there seems to be this power source within this forward development. It appears as if there is either something pushing or pulling all of life forward into complexity, freedom, and fullness.

It is as if there is this cosmic engine that is powering all of life and its development.

A gravitational pull of grace.

A universal drive.

A cosmic will.

One writer calls this "the creative advance into novelty." Another philosopher refers to this drive as "eros." And yet another names this process "Spirit-In-Action."

As Christians, what do we call this?

We can't say that Jesus is responsible for that unfolding can we? It is hard for me to imagine that behind the cosmic curtain is a 33 year old Jesus of Nazareth in a tunic, micro managing the universe and placing stars in different places and making decisions about how the human brain is supposed to grow next.

Although that does sound hilarious.

If we only say God—which in and of itself is appropriate—it does not always provide the conceptual and experiential link with the life and story of Jesus.

If it would be wildly inaccurate to say Jesus is in control of this evolutionary path—and I believe it would be—how does this fueling energy relate to that which was fully present in and alive as Jesus?

So when Richard Rohr asks the question, "What if Christ refers to an infinite horizon that pulls us from within and pulls us forward too?"

He is pointing us in the helpful direction that liberates our imagination to not only see Christ as that which holds all things together, but also as this infinite and universal drive that has been loving this universe into and through existence from the very beginning.

Remember.

This Christ is The Eternal Word from John 1.

That which was "with God and was God."

Through whom "all things were made."

The one the "world was made through."

Can you begin to see how much sense this makes and how meaningful and beautiful it is?

How does the Concrete Jesus fit into an understanding of reality that understands from subatomic particles to the most complex forms of biological life, this is all energy being attracted to each other in relationship?

Well.

From the beginning, this universe is the outpouring of The Christ who alone holds all things together.

How do we speak of a life committed to the way of Jesus in a world with these emerging cosmologies providing a unified vision of the unfolding of the universe since the Big Bang?

Easy.

It is The Christ who the world was made through and continues to be made and re-made through today.

The incarnation of Jesus may have began two thousand years ago in Palestine.

But the incarnation of Christ began 13 billion years ago in the explosion of The Big Bang.

We can see this beautiful evolutionary unfolding taking place through the sacred history of the universe as a whole. From the birth of our world to the present, we can see this development happening at a macro level.

What is also just as fascinating is recognizing how this growth happens through the evolution of human consciousness at a micro level. And as a Christian, it is astonishing to see this evolutionary flow of The Christ on display in the Bible itself.

Yes.

The Christ energy that gave birth to the universe and inspired biological development at every level is also at work in the expansion of human consciousness expressed in the Bible.

Let's explore a few moments in the unfolding narrative within the Scriptures to see this expansion taking place.

In the book of Hosea, the prophet carries the Word of The Lord and says,

"In that day," declares the Lord,
"you will call me 'my husband';
you will no longer call me 'my master.' (Hosea 2:16)

A bit of context.

Hosea is a minor prophet living in the 8th Century B.C. He is speaking in a relational environment that was defined by unfaithfulness of the Israelites, and in a political situation that has led God to actually feel betrayed by the people.

And in this tumultuous relational moment, when vengeance on behalf of the god figure would be assumed by the theological and historical consciousness dominant at the time, what is it that God says to the people?

There will come a day when you will no longer call me master, you will call me husband.

You used to call me my master.

Now you will call me my husband.

This Word from The Lord presupposed that the Israelites had called upon the name of the Lord with this term master—a view of God that was influenced and shaped by the cultural context.

The word master here is actually the Hebrew word Ba'al.

Ba'al was actually a god that was believed in and worshipped in surrounding cultures.

Ba'al was a violent and dangerous god who demanded sacrifices from the people in order for them to trust they were safe.

Ba'al reflected and expressed an old way of viewing God that was not hopeful or loving.

The people used to see God as a master, but now they are supposed to see him as husband. They used to see God as distant, controlling, and manipulative, but now they are invited to see God as close, loving, and faithful. Their understanding of and relationship with God was supposed to change.

And the Bible says God was initiating the change.

Christ was at work calling the Israelites into a future with a more loving, more safe, and more trustworthy vision of the God who was with them. The same divine and dynamic energy that was operating in the Big Bang and pulling the universe forward for 13 billion years was also actively beckoning the Israelites ahead in the story of Hosea.

Let's look at one more story.

Paul was a man known for his unflinching commitment to the way of Jesus, unmatched devotion to the church, and ongoing influence in the life of the church.

But before Paul was Paul, he was Saul.

And Saul was a religious terrorist.

This man was what we would now refer to as a fundamentalist extremist who was not only rigidly devout to his own tradition, but willing to defend or advance his tradition through violence.

The defining moment in his journey took place while on the road between his actions of harassment and imprisonment of Christians. In the middle of his mission against those proclaiming the resurrection of Jesus, Paul had encounter with the resurrected Christ.

This is how he describes this experience when he was writing to the church in Galatia.

> *"For you have heard of my previous way of life in Judaism, how intensely I persecuted the church of God and tried to destroy it. I was advancing in Judaism beyond many of my own age among my people and was extremely zealous for the traditions of my fathers. But when God, who set me apart from my mother's womb and called me by his grace, was pleased to reveal his Son in me so that I might preach him among the Gentiles, my immediate response was not to consult any human being."*

What is the most interesting to me about Paul's description of this transformative encounter with Christ is the word reveal he uses to name this happening.

The word reveal here is the greek word *apokalýptō*.

Which means to uncover.

Or unveil.

Or bring to light.

Or to uncover what was previously hidden or obstructed.

Remember.

Saul was not a person who did not believe in God. Saul was a recognized Jewish leader who had given his life to The Torah. He was already a person who lived by faith and trusted in God.

So this revealing for Saul was not a revealing *that* God was, it was a revealing about *who* God was. Paul already believed in God passionately, and then God revealed Himself more. Spirit uncovered depths and turned the lights on so Paul could see with more clarity, and as a result his view of God was radically changed.

Paul went from a narrow and exclusive view of God that came from his tradition, to a wider and more inclusive view that was revealed in Jesus.

Paul's growth shows us you don't have to change your belief in God to change your beliefs about God.

Besides Jesus, the most influential voice in the history of our faith became who he was and did what he did because he allowed his view of God to change. Christ was at work on that famous road to Damascus calling Paul into a future that transformed his understanding of God and radically expanded his vision of humanity.

Furthermore, in this same letter Paul would make what some believe is the first recorded claim for the equality of humanity when he said, "There is neither Jew nor Gentile, neither slave nor free, nor is there male and female, for you are all one in Christ Jesus."

Christ is always present luring humanity ahead by increasing our ability to see complexity, widening our imagination for inclusivity, and guiding us to a broader and deeper experience of freedom.

Christ is present in the book of Genesis showing us that this is all moving forward.

Christ is present in the words of the prophet Hosea calling humanity further in their understanding of God and their relationship with Him.

And Christ is present in the transfiguration of the apostle Paul's imagination for Christ, humanity, and oneness.

One of the most beautiful and encouraging things about the story of the Bible is the way it fits into our evolutionary framework biologically, psychologically, and cosmologically.

Of course the universe has been unfolding with intentionality from the beginning. This is the Cosmic Christ.

Of course humanity is evolving through a shared journey toward further complexity, depth, and freedom. This is the Cosmic Christ.

And of course the Bible aligns with this universal evolutionary momentum, this is the same Christ at work in the story of the people of God.

This is why whenever people resist change, they are fighting the forward moving flow that has been this universe's birthright from the very beginning.

Calling Out

When I was in my 20s, I had lunch with Rev. Dr. Jeremiah Wright.

Some people may hear this name and think, why does that name sound familiar? Or, I kind of remember that name but am not sure who that is.

Dr. Jeremiah Wright exploded on the broader political scene in 2007-2008 because of his connection with then presidential candidate Barack Obama. Wright was Obama's former pastor at Trinity United Church of Christ in Chicago, and a steady prophetic voice for justice and advocate for the liberation of Black people under the oppression of the United States of America.

And when one of his sermons started to circulate on Youtube, whiteness itself shuddered and shrieked through rage and denial in the media.

On April 13, 2003, Dr. Wright preached a sermon at his church that would have made the biblical prophet Jeremiah himself ask, "are you sure you want to say that?"

At the end of this sermon, Wright demonstrated the power and colonizing reach of the British Empire, and how it eventually failed. He talked about the German, Russian, and Japanese governments, and how they eventually failed as well.

No big deal so far right?

A pastor talking about other nation's pursuit of power and oppressive tactics, and their eventual demise. We're okay with that.

But then he begins naming the ways in which the U.S. government had also been oppressive and failed. Wright claimed,

when it came to the treatment of Indigenous people, the U.S. failed,

when it came to the treatment of Japanese people, the U.S. failed,

and when it comes to the treatment of African people, the U.S. failed.

Okay.

Wright was entering into different territory because now he was not just speaking of the injustice and failure of other governments, but the perpetuation of injustice, violence, and the failure of the United States.

Not too provocative yet, but the temperature was definitely being turned up.

But Wright did not stop there. He continued to trace the historical legacy of oppression, mistreatment, and the dehumanization of Black people in the United States of America. And as this trajectory built to a crescendo, Wright emphatically proclaimed,

"And then wants us to sing, God Bless America...no...not God Bless America, God damn America. That's in the Bible. For killing innocent people. God damn America for treating her citizens as less than human. God damn America as long as she tries to act like she is God and she is supreme."

God.

Damn.

America.

As you can imagine, this statement created a wave of reactions from conservative white voices.

One such reaction came from the Vice President at the time, Dick Cheney, when he said in a response, "I thought some of the things he said were absolutely appalling...but I think, like most Americans, I was stunned at what the reverend was preaching in his church and then putting up on his Web site."

Here's the thing.

This reaction is understandable and makes complete sense for someone who holds a traditional view about America, and operates within a conventional Christian framework.

If you believe America is fair, kind, and just, it's appalling to say that it has killed innocent people or treated any of its citizens as less than human.

If you believe America is a Christian nation who is more concerned with submitting to the power of the gospel than it is grasping onto its own power, it is absurd to even imply that it ever attempts to usurp God or act as a supreme being.

And if you believe America is a benevolent force sent by God for the sake of the world through manifest destiny, it is shocking to ever fathom that God would damn America in any way.

So if you believe any version of that America, then shock and offense make perfect sense.

But Rev. Dr. Michael Eric Dyson had something fascinating and insightful about this collective reaction. Dr. Dyson commented that,

"...it is shocking that it was shocking that what Rev. Wright said was shocking."

Rev. Wright calls out the well documented injustice and violence of our nation toward people of color, and says, "God damn America" for these acts. Then the collective conservative white response is shock and outrage. And then one of the most prominent public voices in the Black community says that it is shocking that people would be shocked.

And I get it.

The God damn America phrase is jarring and unsettling for people.

But if it is offensive and shocking for someone, I have to ask:

Does God bless America for enslaving, brutalizing, and dehumanizing Black people? Does God bless America for controlling actual human beings? Does God bless murder? Does God bless unspeakable forms of violence, rape and the systematic dismantling of the family in Black communities that was normalized through the institutionalized white supremacy and the system of slavery that helped build our country? Is the lynching of Black bodies a sign of blessing?

Does God bless the demonization of and degradation to the indigenous people of our land?

Does God bless the internment camps that Japanese people were forced into?

(And as a side note: maybe the rise of the United States as a global super power has nothing to do with God blessing America, and everything to do with how cycles of violence, colonization, and power work in our world.)

I mean.

What is more egregious to say?

God damn America for murdering innocent indigenous people or God bless America for murdering them?

God damn America for treating Black people as less than human (which is actually written in the constitution by the way), or God bless America for dehumanizing an entire group of people made in the image of God?

Is it more shocking to hear someone say God damn America for the institutionalized white supremacy that is in the very DNA of our nation, or God bless America for violently crushing anyone who does not fit their version of the ideal (meaning white) American?

While some people ask how could he say "God damn America?!" people on the underside of power might be thinking, "How could you ever say God bless America?!"

If in any way a Black preacher preaching a sermon like this, or a Black leader making a statement like that shocks you...

maybe you need to be shocked.

Or jarred.

Or jolted.

Or unsettled.

Jarred out of thinking that everything is okay in our country.

Jolted enough to see beyond the myth of American exceptionalism that makes it impossible to be honest about the dark side of our nation's past.

Unsettled so your imagination can be loosened up enough for an alternative vision of the truth offered by those who have not benefitted from the status quo.

In reference to this kind of confrontation of imaginations, Andre Henry wrote, "It's good for them to encounter Black anger because it undermines the big lie that everything is alright."

This is what prophets do.

They use powerful and provocative language to undermine the big lie that everything is alright. This is why those in power never want to hear from prophets. They are too comforted by the lie to face the truth.

Danté Stewart said that "truth is the beginning of liberation." And while riding through the hills of Vietnam together fifteen years ago, my father-in-law—who is a refugee that escaped Vietnam in 1979— told me "The truth is always a painful truth. But it's still the truth."

We don't want the truth of prophets, but we need prophets.

And also.

Let's not forget.

Jesus was a prophet.

The towering rabbi Abraham Joshua Herschel wrote, "God is raging in the prophet's words."

If this is true, we have to ask the question: are there places in the gospels where you can sense and feel this rage in the words of Jesus? Does Jesus dare to utter those haunting and holy words that disrupt the status quo and shock the social imagination that has been rocked to sleep by the principalities and powers?

To be very clear, the answer is yes.

Jesus' first public teaching in the gospel of Luke began with him quoting the prophet Isaiah,

> "The Spirit of the Lord is on me,
> because he has anointed me
> to proclaim good news to the poor.

He has sent me to proclaim freedom for the prisoners
and recovery of sight for the blind,
to set the oppressed free,
to proclaim the year of the Lord's favor." (Luke 4:18-19)

Which was then immediately followed by Jesus saying, "Today
this scripture is fulfilled in your hearing."

So Jesus references one of the prophet's words about proclaiming good news to the poor, liberating prisoners, giving sight to the blind, and setting the oppressed free. And he concludes this radical social and political proclamation by essentially saying, "Oh yeah...this is all happening through me."

And people try to kill him.

In Matthew 23, Jesus was speaking to his disciples and to the crowds about the teachers of the law and the pharisees and their hypocrisy and obsession with power. We have to remember that Jesus talking about the teachers of the law and pharisees back then was him addressing some of the most public and recognizable religious leaders of the day.

So for us now.

Think celebrity pastors.

Big name Christian writers.

The religious names most associated with big platforms, political power, and cultural status.

It is critical to make this imaginative leap so our hearts and minds can attempt to register how the nature of Jesus' words might immediately and viscerally impact people today.

And what are some of the things Jesus says about the established religious leadership of his day?

"...But do not do what they do, for they do not practice what they preach. They tie up heavy, cumbersome loads and put them on other people's shoulders, but they themselves are not willing to lift a finger to move them. (v. 3-4)

"Everything they do is done for people to see..." (v. 5)

"Woe to you, teachers of the law and Pharisees, you hyp-ocrites!" (v. 13)

"You shut the door of the kingdom of heaven in people's faces. You yourselves do not enter, nor will you let those enter who are trying to." (v. 13)

"...You travel over land and sea to win a single convert, and when you have succeeded, you make them twice as much a child of hell as you are." (v. 15)

"Woe to you blind guides!...You blind fools!" (v. 16, 17)

"...You give a tenth of your spices—mint, dill and cumin. But you have neglected the more important matters of the law—justice, mercy and faithfulness." (v. 23)

"...you hypocrites! You clean the outside of the cup and dish, but inside they are full of greed and self-indulgence." (v. 25)

"You snakes! You brood of vipers! How will you escape being condemned to hell?" (v. 33)

And you thought Jeremiah Wright took it too far! Jesus was ruthlessly confronting the fragile powers that were in place with the radically upending potentialities of the Kingdom of God.

This was not a generic soliloquy given by an abstract Jesus that somehow can be interpreted as personal or simply spiritual. No! This was the status quo challenging, demon exorcising, socially liberating Jesus who was more concerned with the flesh and blood lives of the people who were being stepped on by the system than he was with the feelings of those who were benefitting from the system.

Dr. James Cone said, "To be Christian means that one is concerned not about good and evil in the abstract but about men who are lynched, beaten, and denied the basic needs of life."

And in that powerful moment, Jesus was showing us exactly what it looks like to be prophetic within a religious and political context of hypocrisy.

And that wasn't even everything Jesus said in that address!

Can you now feel God raging in the words of Jesus like Heschel said God does in the words of prophets? Can you see how clearly Jesus fits in and continues the daring legacy of the prophets in His Jewish tradition?

In the gospel of Luke, the writer even says directly, "...He was a prophet, powerful in word and deed before God and all the people." (v. 19)

The prophets don't create crisis.

They name the crisis.

This is exactly what Jesus was doing then and still what following the way of the Concrete Jesus looks like now.

SIX

Experience and Embodiment

Experience

You can have a direct experience of God without having the "right" beliefs about God.

Or even believing in God.

I am usually not that direct. But I felt like making that simple but provocative point as clearly as I could to begin.

Now, a story. I had just parked our Toyota Rav-4 next to our other parking space which was occupied by my wife's fifteen year old Scion xB. This faithful car no longer ran and had essentially functioned as storage for the church we led for the final five years of its existence.

(I remember having to jumpstart this old car multiple times just to make it to church on one Palm Sunday morning. The connection between Jesus riding into Jerusalem on a donkey, and me, as the lead pastor driving to church in an old car that barely worked and needed to be jumpstarted in order to move was not lost on me. I'm still not sure if I was the jackass or the Jesus figure in that moment. Hopefully a little of both.)

On this day, after I got home and parked my car, I unbuckled my three year old son from his car seat, picked up his sleeping body, and carried him toward the automated entrance to the building. As he slept peacefully by nestling his head into the space between my neck and shoulders, I relaxed into the subtle beauty and quiet power of the moment and thought to myself,

"This is The Christ."

Fullness of Spirit and matter.

The simple feeling of being.

The miracle of enough.

This is the subtle transcendent power of being present.

And it is us.

Awake.

Aware.

Appreciative.

Haven't you experienced your own versions of this before?

Sitting on the beach during a sunset with friends, grateful and amazed at life itself. Walking amongst the silent voices of the trees as they share all of their secrets with you. Enjoying at a table filled with love, food and wine reminding you that the only walls that exist between heaven and earth are the ones that we normally allow to remain in place around our fragile hearts.

The wisdom teacher Adyashanti talks about "the energetic signature of Christ."

The energetic signature of Christ.

So good.

Whether carrying our child, watching a sunset, or simply being awake to the gift of connection, regardless of what we believe about God or whether we are invoking the name of Jesus, the energetic signature of Christ is validating the wholeness of the experience.

The Presence of God is present with or without the name of Jesus.

The fullness of life can be experienced in any moment regardless of what you believe about God.

Anybody at any time can awaken to and be embraced by the miracle of what is.

If this is not possible, then what exactly are we saying?

Does God withhold Himself from people based on what they currently think about Him?

Is there a lack of love present to a person because the name of Jesus is absent from them?

Is awakening to unconditional love limited to people who pass an orthodoxy test from the church?

If so, doesn't that sound kind of petty? Isn't it egocentric if someone is only willing to give everything they have for the sake of others if their name is praised and they are given credit?

Wait a minute. That actually sounds more like us than it does God doesn't it?

Does God need the credit to be fully present? Is our world filled with the abundance of Spirit? Are we held together by the self-giving nature of love?

Or is God like us?

And does the name Jesus always need the credit?

Let's move from the experience of the universal love of God without the "right" beliefs and think more specifically about following Jesus.

In Mark 8, Jesus asked his disciples,

"Who do people say I am?"

The disciples replied, "Some say John the Baptist; others say Elijah; and still others, one of the prophets."

After hearing this answer, Jesus then asked, "Who do you say I am?"

Peter replied, "You are the Messiah."

Which of course, was followed by Jesus talking about the inevitability of suffering and the cross, which was then followed by Peter rebuking him in front of the other disciples, which was ultimately concluded with Jesus calling Peter Satan.

The disciples experienced the presence of Christ for years while they were with Him. I mean, they literally were following Jesus. They were as close to the Divine as they could be and yet they did not what to believe exactly.

They were close to Jesus.

They were in the presence of God.

They were giving their life to the Path.

But they were unable to give a cohesive and accurate explanation of their beliefs about who Jesus was or what exactly he was doing, or how he was doing it.

So were they not Christians?

Did they not directly experience the presence of God?

Were they not open and committed to the way of Jesus?

The disciples demonstrate that proximity to the Divine and our beliefs about God are not the same thing. Our experience of God is more essential than our explanation about God. Our own experience of God and life, along with the unique journey of the disciples brings us all the way back to the first point I made.

You can have a direct experience of God without having the "right" beliefs about God.

Now let's briefly look at Paul's story of awakening and conversion

In Acts 9, the writer reports,

"As he neared Damascus on his journey, suddenly a light from heaven flashed around him. He fell to the ground and heard a voice say to him, "Saul, Saul, why do you persecute me?"

"Who are you, Lord?" Saul asked.

"I am Jesus, whom you are persecuting," he replied. "Now get up and go into the city, and you will be told what you must do." (Acts 9:3-5)

Paul's foundation of faith in Christ was not orthodox beliefs, it was authentic experience.

It's not dogma, it's depth.

It's not a belief system, it's an ever present awareness.

It's not about religion, it's about alignment with reality.

The revolutionary spark of our faith cannot be reduced down to beliefs and ideas we carry with us in our rational minds. Faith is alive in our bones, awakened in the center of the heart, and naturally moves through and as our bodies.

In Paul's most defining moment, he would not have been able to explain what it means to believe like a Christian, but he could bare witness to the direct realization of Christ.

Which is why the transformative questions are

Not what do you believe, but do you know?

Not which label do you use, but are you loved?

Not what are the details of your explanation, but what is the depth of your experience?

The Cosmic Christ does not require you to be able to understand the entire story of Jesus in order to surrender to the wholeness of life available in God.

If we are going to say that experience is at the heart of a life lived in tune with the Cosmic Christ, we need to talk about beliefs and bodies.

Can you dare to see and experience your body as the sacred text that it is?

When the writer of 2 Timothy is finishing this letter, he concludes by sharing about the power of Scripture. He claims it is powerful because it is "God-breathed" (2 Tim 3:16).

Or inspired.

Or breathed out by God.

Or written by the Spirit.

Regardless of the translation of this phrase of it in English, the two words used to describe this process are God and breath. The writer is making the profound claim that it is God breathing the Scriptures out, or breathing life into them that provides them with the power to shape our lives into an ongoing expression of Christ.

Genesis 2:7 also provides this provocative and poetic image of what makes a human being. "Then the Lord God made man from the dust of the ground. And He breathed into his nose the breath of life. Man became a living being." Again, we see the power of God breathing.

What makes a person alive? The breath of God.

What makes the Scripture so powerful? The breath of God.

All Scripture is God-breathed, and so are you.

From the very moment I was born again, the primary sacred text for my spiritual journey and life with Christ was my own experience. The Bible came later. While the Scriptures became a source of authority initiating me into the story of God and concretizing the life and path of Jesus, the primary authority for my life with God was

my body,

my heart,

and my mind.

This is where the ultimate authority and transformative presence of the Spirit of God lived.

I learned how to read the sacred text of my own heart. I developed the ability to listen to the Spirit of God within me. I cultivated the interior instruments that enabled me to tune in to how the Cosmic story is being written in, through, and as my own life. I lived with the grounded permission to make decisions about my own life.

My body is a sacred text.

And so is yours.

Adyashanti says, "The important thing is not what we believe about the story, but whether we have the capacity to allow it to live within us, so that the story starts to speak to us in a way that's unique to us alone."

The immanent presence of the Cosmic Christ means that you can learn to read the sacred text of your own heart. You can listen to the Spirit of God within you. You can discern how the Cosmic Story is unfolding in, through, and as you. And it means that you can make inspired decisions to imagine alternative futures that are good for the world and good for you.

Paul had to trust revelation beyond the words of a page.

Jesus had to actually live the fullness of resurrection Himself.

And you can receive revelation and trust resurrection for yourself as well.

Embodiment

The Nicene Creed.

The Apostle's Creed.

These defining statements from the early church not only clarified what the Church believed in the 4th Century, they continue to help billions of people make sense of what it means to be a Christian in the 21st Century.

One theologian claims they are "affirmations of the confessing church that capture the very essence of Christian thought and faith."

Another states, "Creeds summarize who we are, they teach us what is important..."

A prominent leader of faith even declares, "It boldly confesses the grandeur of authentic Christianity..."

The conventional imagination sees the creeds as capturing the essence of our faith, summarizing who we are, and proclaiming the greatness of what being an authentic Christian looks and feels like.

Regardless of historical and geographical location, denomination, or whatever flavor of Christianity you prefer, these creeds have had some of the most significant influence on our identity as followers of Jesus. They have provided guardrails for the peculiar and particular path of Jesus. They have established the dynamic, yet solid riverbanks for the river of the Spirit flowing in the church historically.

These statements of faith are foundational for what it means to be an orthodox Christian.

And yet interestingly enough.

Neither of them say anything about following Jesus or his liberative ministry.

They talk extensively concerning what to believe about God. They extensively communicate the structure of beliefs we are supposed to have about Jesus. They just fail to mention anything substantive about the real life of Jesus.

Nowhere in the creeds do we encounter any reference to

love,

justice,

and liberation.

If our "identity documents" say nothing definitive about the earthy and embodied life of Jesus, then they say nothing about defining our embodied life as well.

The Creeds only speak of our beliefs, and say nothing about embodiment.

So, what's the point of this observation?

Why does this matter?

Well, what danger could become of a religious tradition when the primary identity documents are completely focused on abstract beliefs divorced from embodied practices?

Kelly Brown Douglas answered this question when she said, "an interpretation of Christianity that focuses on God's coming from heaven and becoming incarnate in Jesus, while sacrificing Jesus' ministry, unleashes the possibility for the emergence of the White Christ."

And Bishop Yvette Flunder demonstrates how this same white Christ is why "Good religious folks, who could sing "Amazing Grace" on the deck of a slave ship or at a burning, beating, or a lunching, were the examples of good moral Christians."

This white Christ, that Brown Douglas names and Flunder speaks of, is the abstract Jesus who does not have the essential capacity to care for those suffering under oppression. These abstract and disembodied creeds tell us what to believe on Sunday morning, not who to care for on Thursday afternoon. The abstract white Jesus of the creeds does not even ask us to be concerned about justice as long as we believe in God properly.

We can be completely indifferent to oppression and utterly unconcerned with inequality and still reap the social and psychological benefits of being an orthodox Christian, as long as we agree with the creeds.

The abstract nature of the creeds leads to such a disconnect

between our beliefs and our bodies,

religion and love,

and being a Christian and following Jesus.

Or, as Brown Douglas puts it in the context of the history of the U.S.A, "With salvation guaranteed through belief, White people could be slaveholders and Christian without guilt or fear about the state of their soul."

This identification of slaveholding Christianity as an expression of how the creeds alone can create the disconnect between our beliefs and what we do with our bodies can easily be expanded into a list of how we see this play out in our own context today.

You can still be indifferent to the oppression and suffering of Black people and believe in the creeds.

You can be antagonistic and violent toward LGBTQ+ people and believe in the creeds.

You can pledge allegiance to white Christian nationalism and believe in the creeds.

And while this may sound surprising, I value the creeds and the historical role they have had in the great tradition of Christianity.

But what I am saying is that they are not enough.

There's a story about a pastor who stood in front of the youth Sunday church at First AME Church, Los Angeles, the oldest church founded by African Americans in the city. When this pastor stood up and began to teach about the Apostle's Creed and had the students read it out loud, a young man raised his hand.

When the pastor called on him, he said, "Pastor, he was born, suffered, and died. That's whack. What else did he do?"

The pastor responded by saying, "He had a phenomenal ministry. He healed the sick, fed the hungry, called out the hypocrisy in religion, and called the church to a ministry of justice and liberation."

The young man, obviously paying close to attention to the pastor's reply, responded by saying, "then why don't you teach us about that?"

Following Jesus demands that we pay close attention to his life.

Faith in Jesus may begin in our mind, but it is only real as it flows through our bodies.

Can you dare to see that your body is a more important location for the Word of God than the Bible?

Fannie Lou Hamer was one of the greatest examples of the Concrete Jesus in the 20th Century in the United States. She is the often unrecognized creator of the the phrase, "I'm sick and tired of being sick and tired." Malcom X once introduced her as "The greatest woman freedom fighter in the U.S." Hamer worked tirelessly for the possibility of democracy despite getting shot by a member of the KKK, getting her house bombed, and getting beat unconscious by the police.

Even after a white police officer tells her, "You're going to wish you were dead" and brutally beat with other officers, giving her life long eye and kidney damage, she still continued to lead, still continued to speak, and still continued to work for democracy.

Her grit.

Her sweat.

Her commitment.

Her faithfulness.

Her love.

That is the good news of Jesus.

So when Danté Stewart wrote, "Faith was not a message, it was a moment of body, of mind, of soul, of Spirit." We can see how Famer's life was not a response to the abstract gospel of the creeds, it was the gospel of the Concrete Jesus in flesh and blood.

KEVIN SWEENEY

On the path of the Concrete Jesus, faith is not about what you believe about God in the abstract, it is about how you embody the way of Jesus in the everyday, dusty, real, messy, felt existence we all share.

To follow the Concrete Jesus of the gospels, the path asks:

Not what have you learned, but how do you love?

Not what do you believe, but who have you become?

Not the shape of God in your mind, but the power of love through your body?

Hamer's relentless dedication to justice demonstrated that faith in Jesus is only complete through embodiment. The real question of orthodoxy is not whether or not you can explain the creeds to the church, it is whether you are going to express the life of Jesus in the face of injustice in our world.

I know this is where theologians might make the conventional distinction between orthodoxy (correct beliefs) and orthopraxy (correct practice). But the truth is that when it comes to the Concrete Jesus, this distinction breaks down because the only beliefs that matter are the ones that manifest through your material existence.

On the Concrete path of Jesus, what you do is what you believe.

In one of the most famous interactions of Jesus in the gospels, a lawyer asked Jesus what the greatest commandment was. And Jesus first responded by saying, "You shall love the Lord your God with all your heart, and with all your soul, and with all your mind..." (Matthew 22:37).

Jesus calls us into the sacred simplicity of this way of being, there is a glaring problem with this idea of loving God and loving our neighbor. But here is the main problem with this concept.

You cannot love God.

Not where you thought I was going is it?

How could you possibly try and love God? Can you somehow try and show affection to God in a way that God would receive it and feel it? Are you able to care for God through your presence? Do you have a way to help God? Is you telling God you love him over and over a legitimate form of loving God?

Kind of strange when you think about it.

We are told to love God, but it seems impossible to do.

We receive love from God. We are perpetually sustained in love by remaining aware of and connected to God. We are cared for and healed by God.

But are we supposed to somehow directly love God (as if the divine needs our love and affection to remain)?

No. You cannot love God.

At least in the way we usually think about loving.

Remember when Jesus was talking about sheep and goats? He told this crazy story about how in the future when He comes in all his glory, there is going to be this defining moment where he separates people in the same way a shepherd separates sheep and goats.

He promised an inheritance to one of the groups of people who were present while he was separating them. And when he described who was going to get this inheritance and why, this is what Jesus said.

> *"For I was hungry and you gave me something to eat, I was*
> *thirsty and you gave me something to drink, I was a stranger*

> *and you invited me in, I needed clothes and you clothed me, I was sick and you looked after me, I was in prison and you came to visit me.'*

> *"Then the righteous will answer him, 'Lord, when did we see you hungry and feed you, or thirsty and give you something to drink? When did we see you a stranger and invite you in, or needing clothes and clothe you? When did we see you sick or in prison and go to visit you?'*

> *"The King will reply, 'Truly I tell you, whatever you did for one of the least of these brothers and sisters of mine, you did for me.'*
> (Matthew 25:35-40)

Jesus offers this transformed imagination that invites us to see the act of loving others as the means of loving God. In this story, the unsettling words of Jesus dare us to see that God's Presence is present as the Presence of others—and even uniquely as the most vulnerable, the marginalized, and the oppressed.

Who were the people in this story who were going to receive the inheritance from Jesus?

Those who fed the hungry,

welcomed the vulnerable stranger,

cared for the sick,

and visited the forgotten ones in prison.

The inheritance was available to people not based on the organization of beliefs about God in their minds, but the mobilizing of their love for others through their bodies. Beliefs are not required to love, should not get in the way of love, and are valuable insofar as they help make a way for love.

We can have the embodiment of love without orthodox beliefs, and we can have orthodox beliefs without the embodiment of love.

And Jesus calls us to love.

Cole Arthur Riley wrote, "You want to tell me to love God? Ask me when I've last eaten."

James Cone proclaimed that "To be Christian means that one is concerned not about good and evil in the abstract but about men who are lynched, beaten, and denied the basic needs of life."

And Cornel West declared, "For me, to be a Christian is not to opt for some cheap grace, trite comfort, or childish consolation but rather to confront the darker sides, and the human plights, of societies and souls with the weak armor of compassion and justice."

These authors, who are writing and living within the same lineage as the liberating Jesus, remind us that the most important location where the word of God is written is not in the Bible, but through the sacred text of our own bodies. And even more specifically toward the lives of the marginalized, the forgotten, and the most vulnerable.

If you want to love God, you can commit to justice with the oppressed.

If you want to look in the eyes of God, they're present in the suffering around you.

If you desire to show God affection, you can show it to the forgotten ones near you who are most starved of it.

Jesus revealed that God's Presence is present as the Presence of the vulnerable.

KEVIN SWEENEY

Jesus does not go around teaching people how to love God. And I can't remember Jesus ever telling people to love Him. But I do remember him telling everyone to love each other. And hidden within his constantly emphasis on loving our neighbor is the means by which those seeking to follow the Concrete Jesus can actually love God.

SEVEN

Joy and Justice

Joy

The lights, music, and warm night time Hawai'i weather created such a magical atmosphere for the long table filled with food, drinks, and the most unique group of people.

This was the kind of table that was graced with the presence of pastors who were courageously leading the church into the future, seekers not sure of what they believed, a couple around 60 years old feeling like God had given them a new beginning, and a young queer couple feeling welcomed by the church and maybe even God for the first time.

And during one of these sacred meals, this 60 year old man and legendary Waimea Bay lifeguard, known to everyone as Uncle Mark—who was new to the church thing and yet loved and welcomed everyone with the kind of heart you would hope every follower of Jesus would eventually develop—said something unsettling and fascinating about his experience at the church,

"It's like hell doesn't even exist."

It's.

Like.

Hell.

Doesn't.

Even.

Exist.

This was one of those special moments for me as a pastor that I knew would make the majority of other pastors uncomfortable or even concerned, and yet made perfect sense to my soul. Other religious leaders may have seen this as an opportunity to correct him or to make sure everyone present understood the historical church doctrine of hell (and how all of the people who aren't like us are going to go there).

But I knew exactly what he meant.

He was communicating that ancient spiritual truth that the great mystics have been passing down quietly generation after generation.

It's all about now.

Here.

This.

The present.

He was recognizing that the gift of the present is what really matters. This unassuming sage was confidently articulating that ancient truth in his own profound way right there in the middle of that table.

It's like hell doesn't exist.

Of course!

Unbeknownst to this unexpected saint, he shared a genius insight into the depth of our shared life with God.

The gospel is all about here.

This good news is all about how good this is.

Or perhaps, what he was insisting was that this whole good news of Jesus thing is all about joy.

Right here.

Right Now.

Joy.

And what if he was right? What if life in Christ is all about joy?

Not winning or being right. But joy.

Not dominating or conquering. But joy.

Not defending or protecting. But joy.

Maybe to be human and to awaken to the unfolding of Christ in our universe is to see that this unified field of life is wired for joy.

And maybe that sounds naïve.

I get that.

But maybe it is also true.

I love Christmas.

No, I really love Christmas. Like, going to buy a Christmas tree and decorate your home the day after Thanksgiving while listening to the playlist you've been refining for over a decade love it.

I love the ridiculous and blatant commercialization of it. I love all of the ways the season unlocks this nostalgic feeling for a time in culture, or even our own lives that may have never even existed. I love all of the classic Christmas movies (I watch a different one each night), how the weather transitioning to the cold takes on new meaning (actually for us in Hawai'i, it is still in the 80s), and please do not even get me started on Christmas music.

I just love Christmas.

And if I understand my adoration of this holiday,

it is because Christmas is about joy.

And this simple, and to some, naïve notion of the joy of Christmas is not merely born out of the sentimentality of consumer culture, it originates from the gospels.

In the gospel of Luke, the Christmas story crescendos in the second chapter. Luke writes,

"While they were there, the time came for the baby to be born, and she gave birth to her firstborn, a son. She wrapped him in cloths and placed him in a manger, because there was no guest room available for them." (Luke 2:6-7)

Jesus is born. The coming messiah has arrived. The long awaited King of Israel and eventually believed to to be the Lord of the universe emerges out of sacred history and takes his first breath. According to Luke's gospel, do you know what the first words were that were offered as some form of interpretive key for what exactly was happening in and through this special child?

"Do not be afraid. I bring you good news that will cause great joy for all the people. Today in the town of David a Savior has been born to you; he is the Messiah, the Lord. This will be a sign to you: You will find a baby wrapped in cloths and lying in a manger." (Luke 2:10-12)

An angel appears in radiant glory to these unimpressive shepherds and tells them to not be afraid, and that this incarnational revelation is going to be the cause of great joy.

What is the outcome of the Christ-child? Joy.

Who is this joy for? All people.

The Christmas story is all about joy.

And joy for all people. Christmas is not about a story of joy for all Christians, it is a story about a disruptive and transcendent joy for everyone.

Joy is bigger than your beliefs.

Joy may be discovered in or through your beliefs, but it is definitely before and beyond your beliefs. And I assume even after your beliefs.

But wait. It gets even better.

The Greek word for "great" that is used here by the writer in the phrase "great joy" is the word *megas*. And *megas* is the origins of the English word mega.

How good is that?

Not only is the first word about Jesus one that claims this is going to make joy available to all people, it tells us that this joy is a mega joy.

Mega joy!

The first word about Jesus is that this Christ child would open the door to an embodied and universal joy always available and ever present to all people. Many people think the Jesus story is only about Christians finding peace after death, but the Christmas story is about about all people discovering joy while we're alive.

To follow the Concrete Jesus is to commit to a path has been cleared out by joy and invites us to joy.

Joy is an atmosphere.

The energy of the Cosmic Christ is like the invisible oxygen that quietly sustains us from without, and the animating flame that burns with vitality from within. The Christ surrounds and fills us, transcends and includes us, and invites us to trust that we will be carried further into joy.

And this is not a new idea.

In 2 Corinthians 8, Paul is in the middle of of a letter he is writing to the people in Corinth. What is interesting about this part of the letter is that Paul is addressing the people who are in Corinth, but he is talking about the churches in Macedonia. He is using this story about the Macedonians as an open door for the Corinthians people to step into and see the possibilities of life in Christ for them.

Paul writes, "And now, brothers and sisters, we want you to know about the grace that God has given the Macedonian churches. In the midst of a very severe trial, their overflowing joy and their extreme poverty welled up in rich generosity." (2 Cor. 8:1-2)

At first, there seems to be an unusual juxtaposition happening in this section.

Grace.

Trial.

Joy.

Poverty.

Generosity.

Normally, these distinct experiences remain split and fragmented within our own being. Struggle and joy remain separated. Poverty and generosity repel from one another inside of us. And the idea of grace does not always seem to fit within the concrete realities of struggle and suffering.

But what Paul is showing the Corinthian people and what the Christ invites all of us to see is that struggle, grace and joy are connected.

When Paul uses the word grace here, it is the Greek word *Charis.*

And when Paul uses the word for joy here, it is the Greek word *Charin.*

So grace and joy both emerge out of the same word and idea in Greek.

This word *charis* means

gift,

or favorably disposed,

or leaning toward,

and carries this notion of Christ freely giving Herself to all people.

Grace is this timeless and deathless power of goodness that everything else is built on. Grace is the sacred womb that all things are birthed out of. And grace is the cosmic thread that is woven through all things holding them together and reminding them how good all of this truly is.

Which means then that joy is simply all of the grace that has been recognized. Joy is what happens when grace has been directly realized in the depth of our own lives. And joy is the atmosphere of a world that knows that the ground we walk on is made of grace.

Grace is the ground that everything is built on and joy is the atmosphere everything takes place in.

Which is why grace is the light that enables the nondual mind to see.

If grace is the ground and joy is the atmosphere, everything else has a place to be exactly what it is without negating grace or eliminating joy. We can accept the struggles that come because the embrace of grace is wide enough. We can include any form of suffering because it does not have the power to change the atmosphere of grace that it takes place in.

Grace creates and atmosphere of joy that can never be taken away and sustains the nondual vision that allows everything we label as bad or painful to arise and have its place in this world.

One of the great secrets the mystics continue to whisper to each generation is "No one can take this away from you."

Take what?

This.

Grace.

Joy.

That which is real.

The Christ.

This is why Paul talks about the "grace God has given to the Macedonian churches."

And why Cornel West says, "I got something the world didn't give me."

And why James Finley talks about "the deathless presence of Christ."

To embrace a life that is welcomed within the Cosmic Christ is to dare to be a fool for joy. While we are embedded in a political context providing ample reasons to be upset all the time, and inundated by intelligent voices making constant anger seem like the only appropriate response to reality, the Cosmic Christ does not deny the presence of injustice. But instead makes room for a crystal clear vision of that which is wrong in our world, while still inviting us to dance in the darkness, since there is still plenty of light.

Christ reminds us of the sacred soundtrack of life that is always playing.

Christ calls us to remember that the air we breathe is the very breath of God.

And Christ does the serious work of calling us into the playfulness of joy.

The Cosmic Christ is the lens that allows us to see that even our greatest battles are taking place on a dance floor.

Justice

I went to a predominantly white Evangelical Bible College for three years and only had one professor who spent significant time discussing issues of justice.

Three years.

Three years in a school who believes it knows the true story of the universe. Three years at a school that is based on the truth of not only the nature and destiny of humanity, but of the cosmos itself. Three years at an institution that claims to have good news for history itself, and there is only one person there that was significantly talking about justice.

Sometimes we're saying something without saying something.

We can communicate essential truths about how we see and relate to reality based on that which we omit from our vision of the relationship between God, humanity, and the world.

So what was this school saying without saying it?

Does this cosmic good news not directly impact the concrete living conditions for the very people the God of this story loves? Does this world in all of its ecological, social, and cultural complexity not truly matter to the one they call savior of this world? Does the lordship of Jesus and the universal power believed to be connected with said lordship not have something revolutionary to say about how power is distributed and people are organized and treated?

Is the gospel not directly connected to justice?

One thing I did not mention previously was that not only did we only have one professor talking about faith and justice, but we had another professor who would indirectly challenge the first professor in class when he was not present.

I remember this fundamentalist teacher going on an impassioned tirade that clearly established a distinction between the gospel and justice that crescendoed with him saying things like this:

"If you have a choice between feeding someone and preaching the gospel, just preach the gospel."

"If you have a choice between working for justice and preaching the gospel, just preach the gospel."

This false distinction between the gospel and justice, my sincere but extremely misguided professor was operating with, is one of the main reasons the church has been complicit with oppressive structures in our country. This conceptual and practical disconnect between Jesus and justice has empowered so much of the church to uncritically remain upholders of a racist and dehumanizing status quo, and a barrier toward equality and justice in the United States of America.

The great Dr. Martin Luther King Jr. said, "Every society has its protectors of status quo and its fraternities of the indifferent who are notorious for sleeping through revolutions."

Without a vision of justice at the heart of the gospel they preach, too much of the church will keep on sleeping through the revolution of Jesus shaped justice and the evolution of Christ in our world.

The gospel of Luke mentions that at a pivotal intersection of Jesus' concrete life, he had "his face set on Jerusalem." (Luke 9:51) He knew where his life was heading, he understood there was going to be a clash with the social and political empire of Rome, and he accepted what that ultimately meant for him.

But before he entered into Jerusalem for this social and cosmic confrontation with empire and evil, Jesus did something that continues to remain unexpected for hearers of this story today.

What did Jesus do that can still jar us out of our unconscious grooves today?

He wept.

In Luke 19:41-42, the gospel writer notes that, "As he approached Jerusalem and saw the city, he wept over it and said, "If you, even you, had only known on this day what would bring you peace—but now it is hidden from your eyes."

Jesus took a moment to see his nation and his people deeply and honestly, and he wept over them.

Have you ever experienced that? Have you ever simultaneously felt that desire for what could be and that anguish over what is, and just allowed yourself to feel, grieve, and weep?

Jesus was weeping over what the Temple had become. Jesus was weeping over who Jerusalem had become. Jesus was weeping over how the people who were called to be a light to the nations, to bless all people, to welcome and show hospitality to the stranger, and to seek justice for the most vulnerable, had become insecure and self-preserving of their own power.

God's heart was for equality, but the people trusted in consolidating power.

God's vision was for hospitality, but the people created a culture of exclusion.

God's intentions were for justice, but the people became oppressors of the most vulnerable.

By the time Jesus was walking amongst the people and preaching the good news of the Kingdom of God, this cosmic and social vision for justice of the prophets had deteriorated into an exact mirror of the culture of empire their ancestors had spent so much energy resisting.

Jesus even began his public ministry daring to call people to this ancient vision of justice that he claimed was now taking place in and through his own embodied way of life.

In Luke 4, Jesus stood up in the synagogue and said,

"The Spirit of the Lord is on me,   because he has anointed me   to proclaim good news to the poor. He has sent me to proclaim freedom for the prisoners and recovery of sight for the blind, to set the oppressed free,

to proclaim the year of the Lord's favor."

Then he rolled up the scroll, gave it back to the attendant and sat down. The eyes of everyone in the synagogue were fastened on him. He ended by saying to them, "Today this scripture is fulfilled in your hearing."

This is Jesus letting people know who he is, the prophetic lineage he is from, and what his message is about.

And in this speech, he talks about how the Spirit has anointed him, he proclaims good news for the poor, freedom for prisoners, giving people sight, and setting the oppressed free.

Jesus' first sermon says I'm here to criticize and dismantle the dominant, oppressive social order, and proclaim God's favor over it all. You can't have the oppressed, the captives, and the marginalized without oppressors, captors, and those who are marginalizing. So when Jesus announces the freedom for people, he is calling to account everyone who is standing in the way of that freedom.

Later in his public life, Jesus was weeping over the way things are, but he began his ministry with this radical call toward justice and the way things should be. This is how the concrete Jesus operates in his vocation and work. He grieves over the way things are, calls people into the just vision of how it can be, and invites us to follow him on the actual journey of living this out.

Jesus' vision of justice that he proclaimed and embodied began right there in that synagogue, and people immediately wanted to kill him.

Why was that?

Why would people want to eliminate the very source of salvation and justice?

Why is the possibility of justice experienced by so many as a threat?

Because justice is a threat.

It is an ancient and future idea of love, equality, and equity that directly confronts any social structures that are organized around power, greed, and insecurity. The Cosmic Christ's power of love expresses itself through Jesus' social imagination for justice. And this vision unapologetically shatters the present with all of its collective egoic impulses to maintain the status quo, and invites humanity to dream of a new way.

In Mark 11, Jesus went into the temple to shut shit down (my translation).

He entered this sacred center of Jewish life with this disruptive, justice fueled energy and began kicking people out, flipping over tables, and quoting their own prophets critique of greed and injustice while doing it.

This would have been a scene.

(You know the kind of scene where upper middle class and wealthy people who benefit from the system are in shock and disgusted when people who have been oppressed are challenging the system?)

You know when they are silent but have those offended postures, and a passive-aggressively holding the people they're judging in contempt?

Yeah.

One of those scenes.

And the irony is that a lot of the people I described are living in the U.S. right now, are often Christians, and the person they would be repulsed by in this scene was Jesus.

(The irony sometimes is so hilarious it makes you want to cry.)

But in this raucous setting, Jesus is not upset and driving people out simply because they are selling goods in the temple (which was completely legal), he is confronting an entire oppressive economic system. A system that was lead by the Roman Empire, through the control and manipulation of some of the religious leaders, and leveraged against the lives of everyday Jewish people.

Jesus was not there to save the souls of individuals from hell, he was there to liberate the bodies of people from oppression. He was not attempting to offer salvation that would lead them to heaven in the future, he was working for a form of justice that would lead them to a better quality of life tomorrow.

This was the status quo challenging, empire subverting, and Concrete Jesus getting face to face with injustice itself.

And what is so insightful about this event is the way two different groups of people responded.

The gospel writer noted that, "The chief priests and the teachers of the law heard this and began looking for a way to kill him, for they feared him, because the whole crowd was amazed at his teaching."

The religious and political leaders in power within the system were enraged and wanted to kill him.

The crowd of everyday people being crushed by the system were amazed at what he said and did.

And although Jesus' vision for justice is a threat to the powerful, it is salvation for the vulnerable.

Following the Concrete Jesus means that we look through his eyes and see how he saw injustice and confronted it in his time, and we look as his eyes to see injustice and to confront it in our time. The Concrete Jesus, the liberating Jesus from the Black prophetic tradition embodied such a radical social alternative to the current ordering of things, that the conflict with injustice during his life was as inevitable as it was natural.

Is it natural for us to oppose empire?

Is it inevitable that we're going to challenge injustice?

On our commitment to the path of Jesus, do we embody such a radical social alternative that our very presence is a sustained critique of and challenge to the way things are?

Whether or not we are merely believe in Jesus or are wholeheartedly committed to the way of the Concrete Jesus will determine the answers to these questions.

EIGHT

Compassion Within and Compassion to The Edges

Compassion Within

The Cosmic Christ is always with us.

God's ever present Spirit transforms us as we finally surrender our most precious illusions, and holds us we begin to face the hidden wounds in our shadow for the first time.

This is one of the most personally liberating experiences we can ever have of Christ, and yet it is always the last thing we trust. For most people, the last part of the path of radical transformation is the descending staircase that leads us to our shadow. The refusal of well intentioned spiritual leaders to hold the pain in their shadows and trust that its power will be exhausted in the presence of Christ is what creates countless dangerous clergy.

Pastors leading for decades and preaching countless sermons on grace, and yet still driven by this relentless desire for approval and acceptance.

The spiritual guru leading innumerable retreats and talking at length about dying to the ego and transcending its needs, while still being controlled by their sexual urges and addiction.

The activist who constantly challenges systemic abuse, manipulation, and power, while unconsciously controlling and bullying the people they work with.

You can have direct experience of Spirit, the wisdom of seeing, the gift of communication, and the organizational drive for social change without ever facing and owning the denied parts of your self that are lurking in your shadow. This is why we can have powerful, strong, and charismatic leaders who are still overcome by dangerous desires and compulsory behavior.

It is dangerous when a person is aware of their power, but not familiar with their shadow.

Which raises a simple question.

How does the shadow work?

The pioneering psychoanalyst Carl Jung claimed that the shadow is anything outside the light of consciousness. During the course of our lives, we unconsciously withdraw awareness and push away material from our sight that is too painful or uncomfortable to face. The problem is that although we avoid the suffering of these realities momentarily, they never actually leave our lives.

The pain we have pushed away relocates into our shadow, sustains its power in hidden ways and ends up steering us in relational directions we do not consciously want to go in. Which is why Jung also claimed that "The psychological rule says that when an inner situation is not made conscious, it happens outside, as fate."

Which is why people normally quote Jung as saying, "Until you make the unconscious conscious, it will direct your life and you will call it fate." Which Jung did not directly say, but it's a clearer way of making the point.

The wounds we have ignored are now hiding in our shadow and controlling us and hurting us and others in ways we cannot see. The lies we believe about how unloveable or unworthy we are that we cannot face, are now dwelling in the shadow sabotaging us every time we get close to the love and connection we need.

This is why, when referring to our painful realities, Ken Wilber writes, "Yet pushing them away does not actually get rid of them, but simply converts them into painful neurotic symptoms."

Our shadow controls us in ways we do not know.

Our shadow drives us in ways we cannot see.

Our shadow leads us in ways we do not understand.

The last thing human beings usually do on their evolutionary path is befriend their shadow, and begin the process of including and integrating all of the parts of our self we have denied.

And yet facing our shadow is where we directly realize the compassion of the Cosmic Christ in our own journey of healing, integration, and alignment. We need to find the alienated, unwelcome, and denied parts of our self and begin to see them with eyes of love—which is actually Christ seeing them through us and as us—and welcome them home.

Before we learn to follow Jesus to the edges of society to have compassion on others, Christ moves to the edges of our own shadow and has compassion on us.

The compassion of the Cosmic Christ means that God remains in solidarity with us in all of our suffering.

The compassion of Christ means

you are never alone in your pain,

you do not have to be overcome by your hurt,

you can always experience resurrection after death.

It sounds manageable and even simple when we read about it or talk about it doesn't it?

But we all know in real life, it is never that simple when facing the wounds, hurt, and illusions in our shadow.

Or easy.

Or linear.

Or anything that feels remotely manageable.

Of course it is never easy in our concrete experience. Opening up and receiving the compassion of Christ is beautiful because of how real God's Presence is, but it is also tragic because of how agonizing the pain is. We only feel the co-suffering of Christ when we consciously experience our own suffering in the first place.

But is there a way not to be able to control or manage the suffering, but at least to have a kind of a map for the compassion of Christ and the suffering in our shadow?

I think there is.

I refer to this journey as finding, facing feeling.

Let's begin with finding.

Finding begins with the question, what do I have to discover?

We cannot receive compassion for that which we are unaware of. The compassion of the Cosmic Christ is always present, but without our conscious beholding of any particular form of suffering, we are unable to experience the ever present Christ in those places we need it most.

Which is why self awareness is always the beginning point.

It still amazes me how many "high level" leaders do not know understand what is happening within them emotionally or psychologically.

I remember when I was twenty-one and in my first year of Bible College, I took a class that was essentially the school's version of spiritual formation. I do not exactly remember what we covered in that class, but I do remember distinctively thinking:

How are you going to teach a whole class on transformation and the spiritual life and never once mention self awareness?

This teacher and pastor spent months teaching about spiritual growth and never mentioned the foundational need for an awareness of what was happening in our interior lives.

How are these kids going to change when they are completely unaware of what needs to change?

We start with finding because the depth of the journey of receiving the compassion of Christ and integrating our disowned shadow elements is only possible when we become aware of what is there.

Now we move to facing.

If finding begins with the process of searching, facing moves us forward by asking the question, what do I have to see?

Self awareness and courage launches us into the interior journey toward our shadow, and eventually we see something and need to face it. You cannot receive the compassion of Christ for something you have not fully faced.

This harrowing experience of facing some of the painful truths we have kept in the shadow for our entire life is where the deeply felt need for solidarity and compassion comes into play.

Perhaps this is why the writer W.B. Yeats made the audacious claim that, "It takes more courage to examine the dark corners of your own soul than it does for a soldier to fight on a battlefield."

Seeing and facing the truths hidden in our shadow is one of the most painful things you will ever experience. This is why when people begin to be confronted by their own shadow elements, they might say things like:

"I didn't want to believe this could ever be a part of my story."

"I could not accept that this was my life."

"I knew one day I would eventually have to deal with this."

The courage to face what is in the shadow and tell the truth about what we see requires us to name things out loud we never thought we would or could say.

"Somewhere deep down, a part of me alway felt unloveable."

"I don't think people really want me around."

"If I'm not helping others, I'm nothing to them."

"I was abused and made to feel like nothing."

"I've always felt like a burden to people."

"Without performing and achieving, I could never be embraced by people."

There is a reason our minds withdraw awareness and avoid the emotional shapes within our shadows for decades. It is because some intuitive survival instinct kicked in when the faces of our shadow started to emerge, because we immediately interpreted them as a threat to our very well being and survival.

Do you see why the compassion of the Cosmic Christ is so essential for our lives as we attempt to integrate our shadow? How can we start to see the deepest truth of our own wounds without the holding and healing presence of something that can sustain us?

But without facing what is in our shadow, we will never receive the compassion of the Cosmic Christ in our shadow, and thus, never be able to integrate our shadow.

After finding and facing, we eventually get to feeling.

This is where shit gets very real.

At the center of the process of integrating the shadow is the question: what do I have to accept?

It is in this inescapable experience of acceptance, that we must feel the full weight of whatever truth we had previously determined was too painful to embrace. This (un)holy matrimony between acceptance and feeling is essential to integration because you cannot include what you have not felt.

Some avoid this altogether.

Others begin to do this, start to feel the intensity of it, and pull back.

Many attempt to bypass the feeling part by going around it, while convincing themselves they have done the true work of acceptance and forgiveness.

But the invitation of the compassionate Christ is to face it, accept it, feel the fullness of it, and trust that the presence of God suffering in you and through you will carry you to the other side.

Imagine this impossible form of acceptance being an object that you can actually take hold of in your hands. You hold it, you bring it into your chest as a sign of pure acceptance. And if you have the faith

to hold it long enough,

squeeze it tight enough,

and let it hit you as hard as it can,

eventually you will exhaust of its power,

and the only thing that will remain...

is you.

This is not a process that is defined by your beliefs about God, it is one that is made possible because of your courage to surrender to the living reality of Christ whose compassion alone can sustain you through this feeling.

You can remain in Christ, know the presence of compassion, and experience the power of healing after you have fully felt your way through.

The Cosmic Christ is the invisible body that sits down with you in those parts of the shadow that feel like they have the power to consume you, and remains long enough for you to know for yourself that you're going to be okay. The Cosmic Christ becomes felt compassion each time you open a door within that hides something that needs to be faced, and needs to be grieved.

This ever present Divine co-suffering not only gets revealed in your pain, but makes itself known even more as the compassionate presence that guides you through your pain, and allows you to see life beyond your pain.

The infinite flow cf the compassion of Christ liberates us from the ego need to withdraw our awareness from any form of suffering within, and empowers us to face and let go of each and every illusion we have held onto for too long.

The Cosmic Christ continues to whisper to each person who has the ears to ear, "trust the darkness, face the pain, and embrace your power to let go of anything that is getting in the way of your life, and Life itself."

Compassion to The Edges

Keep your eyes on Jesus.

You ever heard that before?

In the middle of a sermon, the pastor wants to remind you about the ground of everything, the sacred spaciousness you collapse into as you surrender, or the mystical anchor that keeps your spirit steady as you are absorbed within the Spirit of everything.

Okay. They probably wouldn't say it quite like that.

But we know what they mean.

And it makes sense.

But also, do they really mean that? If we actually take a second to think about this as it is logically extended, are you sure we're supposed to keep our eyes on Jesus? Isn't is possible that if we keep our eyes on Jesus, we might end up missing out on those he kept his eyes on?

They say it's about about Jesus, but Jesus kept insisting it was all about your neighbors.

They say everything is for the glory of God, but Jesus kept insisting it's about the care for the marginalized.

They keep focusing on the power of God, but the Scriptures sustain attention on the vulnerability of the marginalized.

Of course I understand the reminder of the preacher who tells us to keep our eyes on Jesus, but perhaps the way forward on the Jesus path is not to see Jesus, but to see who Jesus sees, and how Jesus sees. But if we keep our eyes fixed on this Jesus, we might end up being all about Jesus, without actually being about the things Jesus was about.

So, if the Cosmic Christ provides a universal compassion toward all of the edges of our own life, the Concrete Jesus calls us to follow him and embody compassion to the edges of society. We have to remember that Jesus' primary invitation to his disciples was not to believe in him, but to follow him.

"Come, follow me." (Mark 1:17)

"Follow me." (Matthew 9:9)

And "My sheep listen to my voice; I know them, and they follow me." (John 10:27)

If following Jesus is genuinely *following* Jesus, the questions that arises are, where are we following him? Where did he go? What social or cultural spaces did he move toward? Who did he spend time with? What was he doing?

The Womanist theologian Kelly Brown Douglas invites us to a womanist understanding of Jesus by claiming, "It does not begin with abstract speculation of Jesus' metaphysical nature. Instead it starts with Jesus' ministry as that is recorded in the gospels."

Brown Douglas is helping us see that for Black women, their understanding of and relationship with Jesus does not begin with abstract beliefs about a disembodied God, it begins with the incarnational God expressed in the life and actions of Jesus.

The question then is not who is God?

But where is God? And how does God act? Who does God care for and protect? And who does God confront and challenge?

Brown Douglas is naming the ways in which oppressed people do not have the luxury of speculating on the nature of God in the abstract, but need to recognize the concreteness of God in the midst of the struggle, suffering, and oppression of every day life.

And where is the nature of this God found? In the life and ministry of Jesus. And what is discovered about this God in the life of Jesus?

God sees and has compassion toward the marginalized.

God sees and has compassion for the most vulnerable.

God sees and has compassion for those who are excluded and rejected,

Or, as Brown Douglas puts it, "Jesus is always on the side of the crucified ones."

In Luke 14, Jesus imagines a banquet table that is like the Kingdom of God, and it is filled with the poor, the crippled, the blind, and the lame. This vision centers those who have been rejected, have no social status, and are not seen as people of honor, and yet are welcomed at God's table.

In Matthew 19:14, Jesus uses children as an example of power and belonging in the Kingdom of God. Jesus brings near and uplifts some of the most economically and politically vulnerable people in their society. He celebrates and draws attention to those who are consistently treated as objects to use, and identifies them as sacred subjects in the Kingdom.

In Luke 4:48, Jesus heals a bleeding woman who had been outcasted by the community for over a decade, and calls her daughter. The only location in the gospels when Jesus uses this intimate and relational term of endearment is for someone who was universally excluded and seen with moral disgust.

Jesus' identification with the marginalized and solidarity with the oppressed is everywhere.

Jesus touches and heals the lepers, he describes the poor, the grieving, and the hungry as blessed, he breaks traditional boundaries to heal, he calls out religious leaders as hypocrites, and he lifts up a sex worker as a teacher. Almost every story he tells is trying to communicate that those who you think are in are actually out, while those who you think are out are actually in. And in the end Jesus was crucified as an enemy of the state right next to other criminals, who he still is open to welcoming in God's Kingdom.

In almost every situation Jesus is in and every story he tells, the marginalized are brought from the edges to the center of the heart and life of God, while those who grasp at the power of the center are mocked and removed.

Which is why James Cone said, "The gospel of Jesus is not a rational concept to be explained in the theory of salvation, but a story of God's presence in Jesus' solidarity, which lead to his death on the cross."

And this is why, while making the connection between the Black Madonna and the life of Christ, Christina Cleveland said, "She is the God who has a special love for the marginalized because she too has known marginalization."

Cone and Cleveland remind us that Jesus did not only choose to identify with the oppressed, but that he too was an object of oppression within the same system.

The Concrete Jesus was in a steady flow and movement toward the marginalized. Jesus was also marginalized within the empire, and because of his compassion to and identification with the oppressed, was seen as threat to the empire.

Now that we get a clearer vision of the Concrete Jesus and how he always began on the margins with those who have been forcefully excluded from the center, let's ask some questions that bring us back to our lives and our culture.

Is this what you normally see defining the presence of most churches and Christians today? Do you see the same movement to the excluded edges of the culture from those who most publicly represent Jesus? Are the most popular churches built on identifying with the marginalized? Are the most visible expressions of the body of Christ standing in solidarity with the oppressed in such a way that their very presence is experienced as a threat to the social and political status quo?

Let's ask a different question.

Is most of the Christian faith that you see in our culture defined by following the Concrete Jesus of the gospels or by merely believing in the abstract white Jesus?

The abstract white Jesus does not require compassion toward bodies, it just demands consent to belief.

But in real time, we are unable to be a Christian without following Jesus to the edges of society in our own context and disrupting the social status quo through our own presence and compassion.

Here's a fun idea.

Tell your friends in church that the Black Panthers can teach them so much about what it means to follow Jesus and embody real compassion.

You see, in the late 60s, the Black Panther Party was socially awake and alive in our culture.

They were calling for the equality of Black people in our culture, and if you take the time to read the ten point program that defined the aims of the party, you may be surprised—because of the misrepresentation of the party historically—to discover how sensible and fair they were.

You know, things like:

Freedom.

Full employment.

An end to the exploitation and robbery of the Black community.

Decent housing and shelter.

Education that is not filled with lies embedded within the institutional white supremacy of dominant narratives.

The end of police brutality and murder of Black people.

That doesn't sound quite so disruptive and dangerous does it? Doesn't sound as threatening or violent as it has normally been portrayed by white versions of the story huh?

And during this movement, one of the major programs the Black Panther Party organized was a free breakfast program for kids. And what began at an Episcopal Church in Oakland in January 1969, eventually evolved into a 45 location program that fed thousand of children per day.

This program is a practical example of what it looks like to follow Jesus to the margins and to creatively extend compassion to those you see who have been forced to the edges by unjust forms of power.

And the U.S. government saw it as a threat.

The head of the FBI at the time J. Edgar Hoover, who hated the Black Panthers, wrote a memo to all of the offices, and claimed that the breakfast program was, "potentially the greatest threat to efforts by authorities to neutralize the BPP and destroy what it stands for..."

The leader of the FBI in the United States of America believed that the breakfast program was a threat to the national security of the country.

Compassion was seen as a threat to the racist system.

Genuine care for the oppressed was disruptive to the status quo of indifference.

Being a loving presence to those on the margins had the potential to expose the dehumanizing treatment of Black children by the U.S. government.

The Black Panther Party's Breakfast program is a concrete expression of the compassion of Jesus. Following Jesus to the edges of any culture does not only empower you to become a site of compassion for people, it transfigures you into a disruptive threat to the social and political status quo that is comfortable ignoring suffering people through its indifference.

Kelly Brown Douglas invites everyone to see that the concrete life of the Jesus is defined by his identification with the marginalized and solidarity with the oppressed. Which means that to give your life to follow Jesus should naturally lead you to a life that stands at the margins, lifts up the oppressed, and confronts any form of power that does not do the same.

Jesus did not begin by building networks with the rich and neither should we. Jesus' ministry was not solely focused on providing personal comfort for the individuals who benefitted most from the unjust socio-economic system, and neither should ours. Jesus did not maneuver to be at the tables that held the most status, he did not manipulate his way into relationships with people who carried the most cultural influence, and he damn sure did not cozy up to political power to try and accomplish his mission.

Following the Concrete Jesus is to make a mockery of the system and to expose the conventional social norms of a society that uncritically upholds the greedy, selfish, and hollow status quo that is at the center of every empire.

And to do so armed with the power of compassion.

NINE

The Cross: Yes and No

The Cross as Yes

The cross has a surplus of meaning.

We are still talking about it and wrestling with this meaning after two-thousand years. This is not because human beings are struggling to discover its one absolute truth, but instead because we are overwhelmed by the excess of wisdom that flows out of this event.

The superabundance of truth in the crucifixion allows this event to take root in various cultures, to be born again and again throughout history, and to keep unfolding its dynamic truth through the co-creative process between God and humanity that defines our world.

Jesus' experience on the cross is like a fountain of evolutionary power and possibility that keeps transforming the world and being transformed by the world.

The cross is also filled with paradox.

It is somehow about death and life.

It is an end and a beginning.

It is a violent act that smuggles within it the greatest exposing of the spiral of violence that has plagued the brutal history of humanity since its inception.

The story of Jesus on the cross is about forgiveness and the love of God. This historical event also unveils the fragility of empire, and lays bare the futility of the collective ego's need to control. It demonstrates the inevitability of what happens to the prophets who confront the sociopolitical status quo, and somehow is also an icon of acceptance.

The cross.

One of the most visually recognizable and dangerously familiar symbols in our culture.

An exhaustive amount of energy has been spent talking about it, and yet, there is still more to be said.

So what does the Cosmic Christ have to do with the cross of Jesus? What does the particularity of Jesus on the cross have to say to the universal human experience? What does the perennial wisdom tradition do with the cross at the center of the Christian tradition?

Let me begin by being very clear about something.

For the mystics and the wisdom tradition, the cross is not seen or needed as a form of sacrifice that somehow bridges a gap between humanity and God. Faith as embodied realization is not a cognitive exercise of agreeing to the right beliefs in order to be reconciled to the God who is somewhere over there.

No.

Just.

No.

Faith is a journey of waking up to the God who has always been here, and trusting this loving Presence as the unmerited affirmation of our lives and life itself. In this orientation of faith, the only boundaries that ever need to be overcome in order to experience union with the Divine are the ones that exist within us.

The cross is the bridgeless bridge that allows us to cross over a gap that doesn't exist so we can fully inhabit the space we're already in.

With that as a starting point, the cross inevitably becomes something radically different than the sacrificial transaction needed between God and humanity.

But if not that?

Then what?

Is it possible to include the cross as central to our Christian story without needing it as a sacrifice to be made right with God or as some form of fire insurance for the after life?

To be honest, I believe it is.

The living mystic Cynthia Bourgeault writes, "Instead of a cosmic course-correction, this other approach envisions the steady and increasingly intimate revelation of the divine love along a trajectory that was there from the beginning."

What does that mean? It means the cross revealed and continues to reveal more about the unfolding truth about God's love that has been true and emerging from history since the beginning.

Something true before Jesus.

Something more true in Jesus.

And something, perhaps even more true for us today.

Jesus even said. "If anyone would come after me, let him deny himself and take up his cross and follow me." (Matthew 16:24)

And what is jarring is that Jesus said this to the disciples before the crucifixion. There is something deeply true about the cross that was true before Jesus was on the cross, while Jesus was on the cross, and I believe after Jesus was off the cross in our lives today.

The cross is not a surprising one-time solution to bridge a gap between humanity and God, it is a never ending bridge we all have to keep crossing on the universal path toward life.

For the mystics, the cross is a yes.

Yes to humanity.

Yes to love.

Yes to life.

This might sound surprising because the cross in its first-century Palestinian context was actually a no.

No to anyone challenging the empire.

No to those who were subverting the social and political status quo.

No to the the kind of love that elevated the poor and the oppressed.

The cross was a political tool of violence intended to put on display the ubiquitous power wielded by the Roman empire. The cross was a brutal and binding no to any version of life beyond the control of empire.

And yet hidden within this inevitable end was the unexpected site where the Jesus revolution continued.

Hidden within death was life.

Hidden within an end was a beginning.

Hidden within crucifixion was resurrection.

The Christian interprets this crucifixion and resurrection relationship as a turning point in cosmic history. Jesus has overcome death, resurrection gives birth to the new creation, and the future of humanity and the cosmos has been transfigured. The mystic says yes to this, then sees even more.

What happens is the mystic sees this particular pattern of death and life in Jesus, then zooms out to a more horizontal view of human history, and sees the presence of this pattern as true for all people.

Life always emerges from death.

A new beginning always come from the end.

New forms of freedom can always be born out of the old.

Resurrection is not just God creating life out of death at that time with Jesus, resurrection is God creating life out of death at all times with you.

But this isn't the final movement of zooming out for the mystic. We step back further to gain an even wider aperture of cosmic history and see that this pattern is actually integrated into the universal drive of life itself. The revelation of God and the nature of the event on the cross is not just true for Jesus in that place, it is true for all of life in all space.

The transformation of consciousness, the evolution of culture, the expansion of the universe, and the story of Jesus are all saying in their own unique way, trust the death because it always leads to more life.

Every no that happens in our world takes place within a larger trajectory of this cosmic Yes.

Every form of death transpires inside of the flow of life and resurrection.

Every single cross—no matter how tragic they are or how much devastation they bring—cannot put an end to the unstoppable love, inextinguishable light, and unbreakable force of the Divine life, that alone defines our universe.

The cross says yes, because it is the most profound revelation of what James Finley calls "The deathless presence of God."

Even in the irrevocability of death, God' presence remains.

Which means life remains.

As we zoom out, we see this death and resurrection pattern present no only in human history, but in the epic unfolding cosmic history as well. And now as we zoom back in our eyes are also enlightened to see the deathless presence of God flowing beyond every form of death imaginable.

The cross is about death. But in life, death isn't just about dying is it?

No, death is about

failure,

relationships ending and changing,

expectations not being met,

illusions being exposed,

transformation,

loss,

facing our deepest wounds,

and so many more micro experiences that we relate to as death all the time.

Death, finality, shattered expectations, and loss can be

personal,

interpersonal,

political,

vocational,

creative,

or aspirational.

We are confronted with death in a thousand forms through the natural flow of life. This is why the mystical seeing of the cross as perpetual affirmation of life is so revolutionary. It is having the eyes to see that what was true for Jesus personally when it came to that death, is true for us universally as we are confronted with every form of death that presents itself to us.

In every death, the presence of God remains.

Which means life remains.

Which ultimately means you remain.

Because you are a part of this very powerful, infinite, and deathless presence that keeps flowing.

Within the heart of the Cosmic Christ, the cross is an icon of life itself saying everything you are afraid of, all of the things you fear, even the worse case scenarios you have imagined can happen to you. And the Cosmic Christ, which sustains life as the deathless presence of God, consistently communicates to the universe that none of that changes anything about how present God is, how beautiful life is, and how real love is.

Which is why Frederick Buechner says "Resurrection means the worst thing is never the last thing."

So, even in the negation of an individual life, or of our individual dreams, or of individual movements, the mystics still see the cross as a yes because none of these particular forms of death have the power to contain or conclude the infinite power of life itself.

There is a loving and sustaining flow of life that was present before the cross and remains after the cross. This is the Christ. This is our hope. This is the true identity that exists within and envelopes all identities as One.

The Cross as No

Conventional Christianity told me the cross was an atoning sacrifice that reconciled humanity to God.

The mystics expanded my vision of the cross as the affirmation of life that is present in every form of death.

And the Black prophetic tradition taught me that the cross was Jesus' ultimate identification with the marginalized, a challenge to systemic injustice, and a divine confrontation with oppressive systems.

(I think I'm going to stick with the second two.)

Assuming that, what does Womanist writer Dr. Kelly Brown Douglas mean when she writes "Jesus is always on the side of the crucified ones."

Is she referring to God's incarnation of solidarity in Jesus to those who were literally crucified in 1st Century Palestine by the Roman Empire? Or is Brown Douglas making a statement that transcends their historical location and speaks to the presence of those who are oppressed and crucified everywhere and at all times? If the answer is more about the latter, then every follower of Jesus must ask the question:

Who are the crucified ones in our culture?

Those who are the excluded.

Those who are the poor.

Those who are the oppressed.

Those who are the politically vulnerable.

Those who are the socially marginalized.

Those who are the culturally overlooked.

If Jesus is always on the side of the crucified ones, who are some of these people in our history and experience in the United States?

Indigenous, Black, Latino/a, Hawaiian, AAPI people. Pretty much anyone who is not white.

Women and LGBTQ+ people. Pretty much anyone who is not male, cisgender, or heterosexual.

The poor and working class. Pretty much anyone who is not upper middle class or wealthy.

I could keep going. So, if Jesus is always on the side of the crucified ones, we would assume that the church, who claims to be the actual body of Christ, would always have solidarity with these groups in our culture as one of its highest priorities.

Right?

Right?

Now, is that what you normally see?

Has the Jesus who has been preached and sung about exhaustively in most churches collectively inspired the majority of the body of Christ to use their resources to protect and lift up the crucified ones?

Has the white church collectively owned and repented for their inhumane treatment and colonization of the indigenous people who were here before the U.S. became the U.S.?

Has the church made protecting Black men, women, and children—who are some of the most oppressed, demonized, and crucified people in the history of our country—one of its highest priorities as citizens of The Kingdom of God?

Has the church elevated the voices and calling of women, relentlessly fought for the equality of our LGBTQ+ siblings, and worked effortlessly to create a safe environment for migrants from Latin America?

If the answer is no—and I believe it is—then maybe the Jesus who is always on the side of the crucified ones is quite different than the abstract white Jesus who remains the mascot for the unjust status quo of so much of white America.

Bishop Yvette Flunder recognized this when she wrote, "However, the vast majority of churches remain extremely judgmental in their theology and conservative in their politics towards people who traditionally have lived at the margins of society."

In the United States, Jesus has looked too much like those in power.

The white abstract Jesus does not identify most clearly with those on the underside of political power, but in those who are in power. Most people do not desire a Jesus who sits down with those who have been pushed to the edge of society, but with a Jesus who sits down at the table with those who are doing the pushing.

Which raises the question.

How can you be on the side of the Crucified ones when you worship a Jesus that is identified with the powers that are doing the crucifying?

Or lynching.

Or shooting.

Or imprisoning.

Or whatever form crucifixion takes in any given moment.

If your Jesus naturally aligns with those in power building crosses, you will remain unable to stand in solidarity with those under power bearing crosses.

But the Jesus in the gospels was delivered in a dirty stable that connected him with all people born in obscurity with no visible privilege and power. This Jesus fled his country because of an insecure and violent autocrat, and knows the same journey that all refugees know when they leave their home for a safer place. The messiah of the gospels was plotted against by religious and political authorities, inextricably linking him to countless revolutionaries, organizers, and activists today who know how it feels to have the powers leveraged against you.

Jesus is on the side of the crucified ones because Jesus was one of the crucified ones.

James Cone even said, "On the cross, God's identity with the suffering of the world was complete."

And

As Bishop Yvette Flunder said, "Jesus was himself from the edge of society with a ministry to those who were considered least."

The cross was Jesus' historical and global act of identification with the oppressed.

But it wasn't just solidarity with the poor and vulnerable, it was more.

While the mystics enabled us to see the cross as a "yes" to the deathless presence of God, the Black prophetic tradition encourages us to see the cross as an emphatic "no" to oppressive systems and unjust power.

To take this one step further.

The cross was not just a critique of exploitative power, it was a victory over that power.

The cross was not just Jesus' ultimate identification with the marginalized, it was his consummate defeat of the system that was marginalizing. The crucifixion was not just Jesus exposing the evil oppression of the Roman empire, it was the beginning of him overcoming the evil that animates all oppressive empires.

Forty to fifty years after Jesus died, the writer of the letter to the Colossians looked back in order to make sense of what was happening on the cross, and he wrote,

"And having disarmed the powers and authorities, he made a public spectacle of them, triumphing over them by the cross" (Col. 2:15)

Disarmed the powers and authorities.

Made a public spectacle of them.

And triumphed over them by the cross.

When the writer—who was living in his own context of empire and unjust systems—plays with this concept of making a public spectacle of the powers and authorities who crucified Jesus, he was inviting the listener to remember what the public spectacles and parades of the Roman Empire would have been like when they came back from battle.

The victorious generals of Rome would return from battle and have a parade where they would claim their victory, proclaim the political and eternal power of their city, and humiliate their opponents by displaying their spoils, captured slaves, and the fruit of their pillaging.

Rome would mercilessly disarm all other powers and authorities and make a public spectacle out of them in their triumph.

And what did the writer of Colossians say about these brutal powers and authorities?

That Jesus disarmed them.

That Jesus made a public spectacle out of them

That Jesus triumphed over them by the cross.

Jesus was not only establishing his universal identification with those on the margins of society, but he was exposing the insecure and finite power of every single unjust, oppressive, and violent power.

The same power that needs to make a public spectacle out of the vulnerable, Jesus exposes and makes a public spectacle out of them. The very systems that dehumanize and strip every day people of their power, Jesus strips of their power. The violent regimes that see inflicting death as the ultimate source of victory, Jesus overcomes, not by inflicting more death, but by defeating death, and thus, their faith in death as well.

The cross is a form of protest.

The cross is a crying out for justice.

The cross is a revolutionary act.

It's like God is saying through the cross, what looks like everything is actually nothing. What looks like power is actually weakness. What looks like status is insecurity. What looks like security is actually just control.

When it comes to empires, what looks eternal and everlasting is temporary and has an expiration date.

Jesus is challenging and exposing the eternal impotence of any form of power, any institution, and any government that attempts organize the world in a way that is not aligned with the Kingdom of God. On the cross Jesus was stripping them of their power and letting the world know that none of these empires are going to last.

Which has something profound to say about how we organize our lives as followers of Jesus today.

Dr. James Cone invites us to remember that "it was Jesus' cross that sent people protesting in the streets, seeking to change the social structures of racial oppression."

And Barbara Holmes reminds us that "As witnesses of God-with-us, the church is called to stand silently at the place where the national powers are crucifying the innocent and waging war against the poor."

The Black prophetic tradition does not have the luxury to settle with merely asking us to believe in Jesus. Belief in the white abstract Jesus does not require us to take seriously the dehumanizing history of our country, the present forms of oppression, or the potential suffering of the future of those on the margins if business as usual remains the same.

These daring leaders recognize belief alone for the impotent tool that it is, and call us to a path that is embodied, sacrificial, and that allows the cries of the crucified ones to make a claim on our lives today.

They call us to follow Jesus to the cross, to stand next to everyone put on a cross, and to lead people forward to a vision of flourishing beyond the cross.

They captivate our minds, touch our hearts, and awaken our imaginations so that we too will stand face to face with any force that is anti-kingdom and have the courage to say no. So that we will be animated by the confrontational love of Jesus to the point that we too have to embrace our own crosses and entrust our spirit into Spirit itself.

Ten

Safe and Dangerous

Safe

It is much easier to get pumped up than it is to actually grow up.

So much of conventional church culture in the United States is defined by victory, triumph, and winning. We sing songs with lyrics like,

"I want to see a victory!"

"Shout out to God with a voice of triumph!"

Or "All I do is win, win, win!"

Actually those last lyrics were from a DJ Khaled song. But, you get the point.

These messages of victory are preached with enthusiasm and intensity. Our songs of triumph are sung with passion and jubilation. The collective desire to win, be successful, and maybe within those hopes, finally be able to feel safe is present and palpable.

And I would even argue is a good and natural thing.

But my question is this, is the nature of this commonly proclaimed victory and security made of the same substance as the safety truly available to us in Christ?

The victory preached about so passionately (I was going to say loudly) from Sunday morning pulpits seems to be about God's power, our will power, and the path of speeding through the valleys of pain and tragedy in order to settle back into our rightful place at the top of the mountain of success.

This is the gospel of winning!

This is the gospel of victory!

This is the gospel of America! (Sorry. I meant Jesus.)

But the mystics have a very different take on this conversation.

Richard Rohr says that Christianity is about "learning how to lose."

The medieval Spanish mystic Meister Eckhart said, "No one gets as much of God as those who are thoroughly dead."

Ilia Delio wrote, "To say "I will not die" is to die. To be willing to die by surrendering to the freedom of the Spirit is to live forever."

Jesus himself told us that "Whoever wants to be my disciple must deny themselves and take up their cross and follow me."

These mystics share this staggering alternative way of viewing life with God, and what it means to "win." For them, real life is found within the experience and acceptance of death. To know the fruit of victory, one must learn to embrace loss. To feel secure in God, we must abandon any notion of security that excludes pain and can not welcome tragedy at its table.

In Christ,

losing is a part of winning,

death is the key to life,

and tragedy and security live under the same sacred roof.

Which is why the majority of "victory" language in the church in the United States is just a form of spiritual bypassing.

The psychotherapist John Welwood defines spiritual bypassing as "spiritual ideas and practices to sidestep personal, emotional 'unfinished business,' to shore up a shaky sense of self, or to belittle basic needs, feelings, and developmental tasks."

Spiritual bypassing is born out of an insecure self that does not believe it has the internal resources to withstand the overwhelming sense of pain or loss looming on the horizon. It feels the need to avoid or "sidestep" hard emotions and any form of uncertainty because its own "shaky sense of self" cannot handle the truth.

Then this insecure self preaches to entire groups of people.

Gives them the gospel of denial and avoidance through confident clichés and glib answers.

And then leads them around every form of suffering and pain on the way to a shallow victory and false sense of security.

(Fascinating how those who are the loudest to preach about the cross set before Jesus are most likely to bypass the cross set before them.)

Here's the thing.

When it comes to spirituality and a life of faith, victory and triumph are not primarily about winning, they are about security. We want victory because we want to feel safe. We long to get to a place where we can trust we are being protected, and can finally rest in the feeling of being secure.

We all want to feel safe.

But for Jesus, life and security were never about being protected from pain, struggle, or even death.

In Luke 9:51, the gospel writer writes, "Jesus sets his face toward Jerusalem." (Luke 9:51)

Up until this point in his life, Jesus had gained some popularity. Jesus had a following, Jesus had some admirers, and Jesus could attract a crowd. But Jesus knew that was not the whole story when it came to his mission.

He knew the truth he was going to speak was going to upset people. He knew challenging a corrupt Temple system that exploited the poor was going to upset the religious leaders who benefitted from it. He knew claiming to be Lord and confronting the power of Caesar and the Roman Empire was going to agitate them.

And when he sets his face toward Jerusalem, that becomes a turning point for Jesus facing the possibility of pain and rejection, and still deciding to move forward.

The victory march Jesus was on was not the expected one that avoided death, it was a new kind that surrendered to the deathless presence of God in and through the struggle. The eternal form of security Jesus calmly embodied was not due to the elimination of tragedy, it manifested from the deep knowing that even in the midst of tragedy, Presence remains.

The Cosmic Christ, unfolding as Jesus, reveals one of the great reversals that the human imagination is still collectively struggling to accept.

Acceptance of death is the key to life.

Maybe this why Frederick Buchner wrote, "This is the world. Beautiful and terrible things will happen. Don't be afraid."

Life tells us that we're not safe. Because we aren't.

Christ communicates that we are safe. Because we are.

The gospel says that these are both true.

And I think this is the good news.

If you were to walk into my home, you would be walking into a condo about four hundred feet in the air. You would see a mesmerizing view that includes the Pacific Ocean, the Waianae Mountain range, and downtown Honolulu.

(You would also see toys on the ground, various kids sports equipment in the corner, and a monkey stuffy hanging from a plant in the corner.)

And on the wall above our TV, next to a couple of framed photos of some of the most beautiful places on our island, you would see three framed quotes. One of them is about the miracle of the present by a Buddhist monk, another is by a thirteenth century Sufi mystic about the divine dancing in our chest, and the third is by a first century ancient near eastern writer making sense of the relationship between Jesus and the universe.

The quote in this frame says, "In him, all things hold together." Which comes from the letter to the Colossians.

In the Cosmic Christ, all things are held together.

The phrase hold together here is the Greek word, *synestēken*.

This word is about:

being with,

standing near,

having union,

or being together.

The cosmic source of all that is arising manifests itself as love. And what does this love naturally do? Stays connected, remains in union, and persists in being close. Which means this ever arising love continuously connects with us and sustains us.

Not defending us from every thing, but remaining with us through everything.

Not shielding us from suffering, but staying with us in suffering.

Not guarding us from pain, but guiding us through pain.

The great sages reveal to us this alternative way of living in this world. We can feel safe in this universe not because we are protected from anything, but because we are connected with everything, and sustained by everything.

James Finley even dares to proclaim that "God protects us from nothing, but sustains us in everything."

That is one of those one liners that is poetically beautiful, conceptually true, and at the same time reveals a devastating truth that your mind will almost completely reject.

To be protected from nothing means you are not in any way exempt from the tragic nature of existence. But to be sustained in everything means you are fully capable of remaining awake and alive no matter what unwelcome expression the tragic takes in your life and in this world.

To be safe in a world held together by the gospel of spiritual bypassing means to be invulnerable. This is a false promise of being protected from tragedy. This is an illusion that subtly communicates that if you're good enough or Christian enough, God will undoubtedly defend you from the worst of human suffering.

In this way of seeing, safety is avoidance.

But to be safe in the world held together by Christ means to accept that you are absolutely vulnerable. Vulnerable comes from the Latin word "vulnus," which mean woundable. There is nothing in The Christ energy that holds all things together that carries the promise that you will not be wounded.

And I wish this wasn't how it was for people.

But to be human is to embrace that you are utterly vulnerable, completely woundable, and still safe because of the union of Christ. Hidden at the center of this living Reality is a place for each of us that will be sustained and remain whole, even as we present our naked and vulnerable selves to this unsafe world.

In this way of seeing, safety is acceptance.

Perhaps, this is why the great mystic, Mechthild of Magdeburg wrote,

"I who am Divine am truly in you.
I can never be sundered from you:
However far we be parted,
never can we be separated.
I am in you and you are in Me.
We could not be any closer.
We two are fused into one,
poured into a single mould.
Thus, unwearied,
we shall remain
forever.

No separation. Could not be any closer.
Fused into one. Remaining forever."

With this in mind, of course we're safe.

The Cosmic Christ situates us in a world where our sacred identity transcends our own individual experience of life. This pure awareness is where we realize that anything we can see is not who we are, because at our deepest level, we are a part of that which is doing the seeing.

This sacred location alone knows that every form of love will pass away except Love itself.

This holy space accepts that each individual presence has an expiration date, but Presence itself is Eternal.

This ultimate identity can feel safe in an unsafe world because it trusts that no matter what happens, Presence is always going to remain.

Dangerous

Martin Luther King Jr. was targeted by the FBI and under surveillance for years. The FBI exerted tremendous amounts of energy with the intent to bring Dr. King down, even wiretapping his home. The FBI tried to slander his reputation, with the head of the FBI, J. Edgar Hoover even referring to King as "one of the most notorious liars in the country."

The FBI saw Dr. Martin Luther King Jr. as dangerous.

Fannie Lou Hamer—who I have already mentioned— was one of the greatest civil rights leaders and one of the most courageous Christians in the twentieth century. Throughout her life as a freedom fighter, she was fired from jobs, shot at by the KKK, and beaten so bad by the police that she got permanent kidney damage. Hamer was also tracked by the FBI.

The police and the FBI saw Fannie Lou Hamer as dangerous.

During the British rule in India, the Magnificat (Mary's words about Jesus) was prohibited from being sung in Church. In the 1980s, the Guatemalan government viewed Mary's words as too dangerous and revolutionary and banned any public reading of it. And after the mothers of the "Plaza de Mayo" put up Mary's words around the capital to bring awareness to all of their missing children during the "Dirty War," in the 1980s, the military junta of Argentina made it illegal for any one to publicly display Mary's words in the Magnificat.

Oppressive global super powers and violent political regimes saw Mary, the mother of Jesus as dangerous.

And of course we know why each one of these prophetic voices was viewed as dangerous.

Because Jesus was dangerous.

All of these courageous voices for freedom and justice were naturally labeled as dangerous by the empires they lived under because of their commitment to the Jesus who was seen as dangerous by the empire and institutions he lived under.

From his birth, Jesus has been viewed as dangerous and experienced as a threat by insecure leaders and power obsessed institutions bent on self preservation. In the beginning of the gospel of Matthew,

"When Herod realized that he had been outwitted by the Magi, he was furious, and he gave orders to kill all the boys in Bethlehem and its vicinity who were two years old and under, in accordance with the time he had learned from the Magi." (Matthew 2:16)

At his birth, Jesus was viewed as dangerous.

During his life, Jesus was seen as dangerous.

And in his death, Jesus was killed as one who was dangerous.

Kelly Brown Douglas reminds us that, "Jesus informed his followers that the Kingdom of God would mean a revolutionary change in the way things were."

And guess what?

It was.

After Jesus preached his first sermon where he centered the poor, liberation for the captives, and setting the oppressed free, religious leaders formed a mob and tried to kill him.

While Jesus transgressed social and cultural boundaries as if they did not exist, intentionally subverted laws for the sake of healing and inclusion, and continuously identified with the marginalized and challenged those in power, institutional leaders plotted against him.

And when Jesus confronted an entirely corrupt economic system being ran through the religious authorities and controlled by the Roman Empire, he was eventually killed as a rebel and an insurrectionist.

Jesus was seen as dangerous.

Jesus was viewed as a threat.

Jesus was a disruptor of the social and political status quo, and as a result had to be eliminated.

Jesus did not antagonize the poor, he irritated the rich. Jesus did not exhibit any oppositional energy toward those on the edges of society, but he was clearly defiant of and challenging to those in power. Jesus never ridiculed or shamed the vulnerable or oppressed, he mocked and exposed the fragility of the oppressor and their tools of oppression.

Jesus wasn't just seen as dangerous or wrongfully accused of being a threat.

He was dangerous and he absolutely was a threat.

The imaginative shape of his vision for justice in the future was a threat to the current ordering of people and power during his time. His relentless identification with the marginalized was a constant critique of a society obsessed with status. His embodied way of uplifting and magnifying the dignity of the poor, coupled with his powerful stories of subverting a status quo that elevated the wealthy, was dangerous for everyone who benefited from the status quo.

If it is true that Jesus and his vision of a justice that centers the marginalized was a serious threat to the social and political status quo of his day, and I believe it was...

Why do we have a church that instinctively aligns itself with power?

Why do we have a church that always seems more comfortable in the board rooms than they do the streets?

And why do we have a church that looks more like the Roman Empire who killed Jesus than the Jesus who they crucified as a threat?

If you do not follow a Jesus that is dangerous to the status quo and the indifference of all who benefit from it, your faith and your churches will uncritically cooperate with the very forms of power the Kingdom of God was a threat to. If your faith is defined by belief in the abstract white Jesus, you will support and uphold the very systems that viewed Jesus as dangerous.

Too many churches preach the abstract white Jesus that promises to save individuals while unknowingly supporting the systems that enslave, lynch, humiliate, murder, exclude, and oppress.

Have you been taught that some of the most renowned founders, leaders, and presidents in our country were also actively engaged in the brutality of slavery?

Are you aware that the doctrine of discovery, manifest destiny, and white supremacy became the justification for colonial actions, and enabled native genocide and the stealing of land to be viewed as ordained by God.

Did you know that countless white Christians were not only present during the lynching of Black people, but were emotionally indifferent to the dehumanization to the point where they were able to have picnics while it was happening.

And let's not forget that the Southern Baptist Convention basically began to uphold their right to have slaves.

In the May 1963 Gallup survey, it was recorded that only 35% of white American adults had a favorable view of Dr. Martin Luther King Jr. And in his famous "Letter From a Birmingham Jail" King expressed his disappointment in the white church because of their lack of support of the civil rights movement.

He said that while assuming white priests and ministers would be some of his biggest supporters in the South, "...some have been outright opponents..."

He unapologetically claimed that the white church, "So often it is an archdefender of the status quo."

Which lead him to write, "Over and over I have found myself asking: "What kind of people worship here? Who is their God?"

What kind of people worshipped there? And who was their God? Clearly, it was not the liberating Jesus of the gospels.

And in the spirit of Dr. King, we can still ask these same questions about so many expressions of the church today.

The church's ongoing exclusion of LGBTQ people and the inner conflict it creates still contributes to a higher likeliness of suicide attempts for queer people growing up in the church.

White pastors today are still signing statements that dismiss social justice, deny the value of feminism and critical race theory, and argue that social activism are not "integral components of the gospel or primary to the mission of the church."

Even as of 2018, 71% of white evangelicals believed that police officers killing Black men are isolated incidents and are not connected with a larger culture and systemic pattern of racism and violence in the police force.

And according to the Pew Research Center, 68% of white evangelicals say that America has no responsibility to welcome and care for immigrants.

And in 2016 and 2024, the most racist, sexist, and morally depraved president in our current day won the election with majority support from white evangelicals and white catholics.

To return to Dr. King's questions in the context of this religious situation today: What kind of people worship here? Who is their God?

I'm not sure about the kind of people who worship here, but I do know that the god that is worshipped is the abstract white Jesus.

And no matter how much the church remains in ignorance because of the truncated vision of the abstract Jesus, or how comfortable it gets relaxing in the penthouses of the empire, the Concrete Jesus is still calling us to be dangerous today.

Cornel West even said that "to be Christian is to live dangerously..."

He claimed that to be a follower of Jesus means "to step in the name of love as if you may land on nothing, yet to keep stepping because the something that sustains you no empire can give you and no empire can take away."

To follow Jesus is to live dangerously.

And if you're never viewed as dangerous to the social status quo or experienced as a threat to the religious establishment, you're not following the liberating Jesus of the gospels.

So what does it look like to follow this disruptive and dangerous path of Jesus today?

Maybe it looks like still committing to a path of peace in a country that has normalized a constant culture of war. It could look like boldly naming the evil of the system of mass incarceration and exposing it for the anomaly and embarrassment that it is—especially for the legacy of the so called greatest country in the world. Maybe it is the refusal to be silent about the institutionalized white supremacy that gave birth to this nation, raised our country, and is still fighting for its place on the throne of our government.

Or.

It could be closer to home in the church.

Perhaps, it looks like more and more clergy who stop silencing their truth as they just keep going on with the way things are in order to keep a paycheck and the peace. Or maybe it means that the choir of voices who keep calling out the abuse of power, the obsession with celebrity, and the corporate metrics that are ruining the public witness of the church needs to keep growing and getting louder.

I know it looks like a growing portion of the church stopping the exclusion of our LGBTQ+ siblings in the name of the most inclusive person in human history.

And maybe if people do that, they just might discover the party that Christ has been inviting them into is just on the other side of the door that the gatekeepers of the status quo have been protecting the whole time.

ELEVEN

Unity and Community

Unity

There's a story about a God who created a beautiful world.

Out of his infinite imagination and through the power of his words, this God placed the stars in the sky, set the ocean in its place, and formed a resilient land that carried the potential to create even more.

This creative Source even provided vegetation and fruit for sustenance, filled this world with wild creatures that all had their place in this sacred cosmos, and even created human beings.

These people had the genius to care for and cultivate the land, and the imagination, like the God who created them, to build an entire world. They could name the animals, take care of everything they had been entrusted with, and enjoy it as well.

Then this God looked at everything They created and said it was good.

But then the first people disobeyed God and God got upset and banished them from their home. This decision allowed for separation between them and initiated chaos and violence in the land. Eventually in His mercy, God decided He was going to rescue some of the people and lead them to safety in another place called heaven, while destroying the earth, and making all of the other people He did not rescue—based on abstract beliefs they carried about Him—suffer in eternity in another other place called hell.

So ultimately, this story of an affirming God who creates this sublime world ends with Him abandoning this world, and only welcoming some of the people He formed to be united with Him forever, while the rest of the people suffer for eternity.

Is that a good story?

Does that sound like a story that is born out of and defined by unity?

Do you think the God of this story is a model for unconditional love and fidelity?

Sure, you might say that this story sounds like a caricature of the biblical narrative. But even in its overly simplistic form, this story does represent the conventional understanding of the creation, fall, redemption arch most Christians have.

Christians go to heaven.

Non-Christians go to hell.

The earth and universe is gone.

Sound familiar?

Exactly. Which is why this familiar rendering of the Story raises two enormous questions:

Does this loving God condemn billions and billions of people to eternal suffering and separation?

And also, what about God's relationships with the world She created and affirmed?

A story about the separation of humanity from God and the disintegration of this interconnected universe betrays the unity and unifying power of the Christ that is so central to the Bible. This story that is defined by the loss of connection, the failure of fidelity, and the fragmenting of reality is so un Christ-like that it cannot be true.

Genesis 1 evokes this poetic image of a seamless reality that does not include a dualistic split between heaven and hell.

In the gospel of Matthew, Jesus speaks of the "renewal of all things."

The apostle Paul claims this divine flow "was reconciling the world to himself in Christ."

And we see in Revelation 21, John's poetic vision of the future is one of unity through the marriage of heaven and earth when the writer notes, "I saw the Holy City, the new Jerusalem, coming down out of heaven from God, prepared as a bride beautifully dressed for her husband."

How does the story end?

Unity.

Reconciliation.

Connection.

When Paul, the great pioneer of the Christian understanding of the Cosmic Christ, reflects on this new emerging vision, he writes that God had "made known to us the mystery of his will according to his good pleasure, which he purposed in Christ..."

And what was this mystery God was revealing?

That God was going "...to bring unity to all things in heaven and on earth under Christ." (Ephesians 1:9-10)

Paul tells these early followers of the way of Jesus that the great Mystery is that this is all moving toward oneness in Christ. This vision not only sees connection within creation and the unity of the cosmos, but dares to see a Oneness that transcends our universe and holds together the finite and Infinite in the same space.

Did you know there is this propensity within all things—down to the most sub-atomic level—to move into relationship? And that at the deepest level, every atom in the universe seeks to remain in relationship with every other atom. Through these invisible networks of atoms and relationships of energy, we can see that the building block of material life is defined by connection, relationship, and unity.

The evolutionary cosmologist Brian Swimme calls this the "Urge to Merge."

It appears the foundational need for connection is built into the very structure of life itself.

Everything has this yearning to move into relationship.

Including us.

What is deepest in humanity—which is the intense desire for connection and relationship—is actually an expression of what is true about every element in the universe. Our world, while commonly interpreted by our minds as isolated objects, is actually a seamless unity of networks of subatomic relationships and patterns.

So when Paul says this is all moving toward unity and that its all wired for connection, quantum physics, the sub-atomic structure of material life, and the universe itself seem to agree.

Creation is about connection.

Our universe is moving toward more and more unity.

And maybe, if we go just a bit deeper, we will see this unifying movement within the cosmos is actually an expression of the truth that every thing we see unfolding in the universe is a part of the One Thing that is unfolding as the universe.

In the beginning, creation was actually incarnation.

Whether we are looking at the biblical poetry of Genesis 1 or the scientific notion of The Big Bang, the Infinite God invested the substance of His being in, committed to give Himself through, and began to take form as what we now know call the universe.

The Absolute unfolding through the relative.

The One manifesting itself through the many.

The Unity revealing itself though the diversity.

This is why when Richard Rohr reflected on creation, he wrote, "The self-disclosure of whomever you call God into physical creation was the first Incarnation (the general term for any enfleshment of spirit), long before the personal, second Incarnation that Christians believe happened with Jesus."

Is it possible that what was true for Jesus in his personal incarnation in a 1st Century Jewish and Palestinian body, was always true for our universe from the beginning?

Let's think about that. First, what does the Christian tradition claim to be true about the incarnation of Jesus?

It is a life where the fullness of Divinity and humanity co-exist.

It is a physical space where Spirit and matter are One.

It is a revelation that the Infinite and the finite are joined in undivided unity.

The mystic does not look at the incarnation of Jesus and claim that it is not possible. Instead, the mystic sees the incarnation of Jesus and proclaims not only that it is true of his life at that time in history, but that it is true for all of life throughout history.

The birth of Jesus was not the first incarnation of Spirit and matter co-existing as One. But if we wrestle long enough with the incarnation in the Concrete Jesus, it has the power to become an invitation to see the incarnation of the Cosmic Christ everywhere. The great saints, sages, and lovers of God have dared to believe that everything the church has historically believed about Jesus is true for all of material life as well.

This why creation was the first Christmas.

Creation was the Cosmic Christmas announcing the birth of God unfolding in, through, and as this universe.

And now to take that eternal logic of the incarnation a step further. The infinite not only expresses itself in the fullness of creation, it is also fully present in each part of creation.

Which means

Spirit is in everything.

And also,

Spirit is in every *thing*.

God is both unfolding through the sum total of everything, and present in the depths of every thing. You can discover Spirit as the animating force and interconnecting thread of the cosmos, and experience God's Presence in any individual part of our world. God's being is invested in every single thing that is arising as a part of the universe, and is also the space in which everything is arising.

Which is why when speaking of the individual person, Rumi writes, "You are not a drop in the ocean. You are the entire ocean in a drop."

Rumi recognized that each human being is not simply a drop in the ocean of God, but that the ocean of God is fully present within each person. And this same connection between the whole and the parts that Rumi was conveying is true not just for each person, but for every created thing.

This is why you can have a profound experience of the mystery of God by being present and beholding a single leaf. Or why you can see the ever present stream of God's Spirit with more clarity when you take the time to sit by a river. Or why the best sermon you ever heard about the death and life pattern came from a tree.

And this is why the Bible has countless examples of the fullness of Christ emerging as and breaking through so many unexpected places of matter.

The Wisdom of Christ is found

in a rock,

in dreams,

in foreigners,

in a field,

in ants,

and in the sky.

Each particular expression of creation is a carrier of and an invitation to the universal and sacred pattern of everything.

So when Richard Rohr asks, "What if Christ is the name for the transcendent within of every thing in the universe?" He is recognizing that the Divine wholeness is mysteriously hidden within everything, and every thing.

Any thing is the carrier of Everything.

The unity of God transcends parts and wholes, the absolute and the relative, heaven and earth, and includes them and embraces them all as One Thing in the Cosmic Christ.

Community

My kids love to watch the show Bluey.

There is an episode in season 1 called, "Bumpy and the Wise Old Wolfhound." In this episode, Bingo, Bluey's little sister is in the hospital and not feeling well. While she is in there, her dad sends her a short movie he filmed with some of her family and friends about a character named Barnacus, who was worried about her sick puppy, Bumpy.

Barnacus was devastated and unsure what to do because her beloved puppy, Bumpy, unexpectedly got sick. Barnacus began asking around her neighborhood to see if anyone knew how or had the power to heal Bumpy. She was discouraged because she could not find anyone to help, until the baker told her to go see the wise old wolfhound.

So Barnacus makes the trek to the tent where the wise old wolfhound was, and asks this guru like healer if she could "magic him better." The wise old wolfhound told Barnacus to bring her a pair of purple underpants (it's a kid show) from someone who had never been sick before in order to make things right.

Barnacus left with a renewed energy to finally find the magic to heal her puppy.

She finds the shopkeeper, requests his purple underpants, but then asks him if he has ever been sick. He said yes, and that he actually has bum worms right now (all of the characters are dogs by the way). She speaks to the baker and finds out that she just had rabies, which of course, she pronounced as "wabies" because she is a toddler dog.

Barnacus could not find a single dog she knew that had never been sick before.

And while she was worried and sitting in the wake of this failed attempt to find the magical underpants she needed to give to the wise old wolfhound to magically make Bumpy better, she had a realization about what she was supposed to learn in the process.

Barnacus said, "Everyone gets sick sometimes...Being sick is just a part of life."

And from that moment on, Barnacus stopped obsessing over finding the quickest way to get rid of her puppy's sickness, and instead started slowly accepting it and moving forward, until one day she woke up and discovered that Bumpy was all better.

She moved from the desire to fix the suffering, to solidarity in suffering, to the acceptance of suffering.

Pretty profound for a kid's show right?

Well.

This wonderful story is actually an adaptation from a famous Buddhist parable referred to as "Kisa Gotami and The Mustard Seed."

In this story Kisa Gotami's son died. And after visiting the Buddha, he told Gotami to bring him mustard seeds from a house of someone who had never had anyone close to them die. She never found such a person, but through the process, realized she was not alone, and that death is a part of life. And she finally transitioned into a space of acceptance.

Bluey and this Buddhist story are revealing the power of stories, solidarity, and embodied compassion in the healing journey. The stories of others' sickness, along with them being sustained through the suffering became the strength for the one struggling in the story. It was not an answer, but an awareness that they were not alone, that sustained them in the path ahead.

Do you know what the Concrete Jesus of the Black prophetic tradition offers to us so profoundly in times of immense suffering?

Each other.

So many of these brave and resilient men and women keep reminding us that the site and source of our healing is community. The writer and mystic Barbara Holmes says that "We are born not only into a wondrous and mysterious life space but also into communities of interpersonal reliance."

Christ speaks to us through the affirming voices of our friends.

Christ comforts us through the divine embrace of our mothers.

Christ reassures us through the hands of our siblings that hold ours tightly.

To remember that we are relationally loved into existence and carried through our lives communally is to discover that the presence of God does not just show up through people, but as people.

And that the Cosmic Christ's energy is not just in other people, it is other people.

Near the beginning of the gospel of Mark, there is a very well know healing story about Jesus. The Scriptures say,

"A few days later, when Jesus again entered Capernaum, the people heard that he had come home. They gathered in such large numbers that there was no room left, not even outside the door, and he preached the word to them.

Some men came, bringing to him a paralyzed man, carried by four of them. Since they could not get him to Jesus because of the crowd, they made an opening in the roof above Jesus by digging through it and then lowered the mat the man was lying on. When Jesus saw their faith, he said to the paralyzed man, "Son, your sins are forgiven." (Mark 2:1-5)

Sounds simple and straightforward.

But of course it's not.

This is because tribal religion is usually only interested in healing to the degree by which it is their own approved of people that are doing the healing. So some teachers of the law get angry with Jesus for healing and forgiving this man, and claim that he is blaspheming God (that's called irony).

Which eventually leads to Jesus completely subverting their understanding of forgiveness and healing, and amazing the crowd in the process.

But.

There is something else going on here that is not usually the focus of conventional readings of this text. Jesus does not just forgive the man's sins and heal his body, he liberates him from his shame so he can return to his family.

We need to understand. Jesus lived in a rigid culture of honor and shame.

Although there are countless contextual nuances to this cultural way of relating, it essentially meant that there are decisions people make and concrete realities they live with that either bring honor or shame to them and their family. If you are doing and being good, you bring honor to the family and remain welcomed. If you are doing or being bad, you bring shame to your family, which can lead to you being shunned and even excluded from the family and from the larger community as well.

Some of you grew up calling this youth group and family values.

(That was a joke.)

But this system meant that a person was constantly required to perform the good to maintain honor, and constantly covering up the bad to avoid being shamed.

Here is an example of how this works and why this story means something so much powerful than we even realize.

Households in this time and culture usually had a trade and worked together to produce. So when you had an unproductive family member, they were seen as a strain on resources, and possibly a great source of shame to the family.

If you did not contribute and produce to the family's health (even if you had a physical ailment from birth that you did not choose that prevented you from making the expected contribution), you were seen as shaming the family, which then had consequences. Which could have even been rejection and exclusion from the family and home.

So by the time we are introduced to this paralyzed man in the story, it's possible that his father threw him out, and also that he left his household to avoid the constant shame he felt in the family.

So now that we've considered this, when Jesus heals this man's body and forgives his sins, what does that mean?

The physical limitations that kept him from working with his family were gone.

The primary source of cultural shame that was a barrier for inclusion is no more.

This man is now able to return to his family, contribute, and be embraced.

And what does Jesus say to this man after he heals him and the teachers of the law are done arguing with him?

"I tell you, get up, take your mat and go home." (Mark 2:11)

Go home.

He told the man to go home because his future of healing and wholeness was going to be experienced in the glorious context of relationship and community. Jesus' forgiveness and healing did not just make a way for him to be aligned with God, it made a way for him to be embraced and healed through his people.

Following the Concrete Jesus leads us into the arms of lovers, liberates us to be seen by friends, and awakens us to be healed through the body of Christ.

Contemporary Womanist theologian Dr. Monica Coleman and author of the powerful book, "Bipolar: A Black Woman's Journey With Depression and Faith" tells her own story of pain and mental health struggles. And in one of the most profound and poetic sections of the book, when she discusses her own path of healing and surviving, she writes,

"God was knitting me. With therapists, medication, meaningful studies, a small church community, a pastor who cared, friends who understood, and a name for my condition, God was knitting me. God was knitting me back together. It was a new way of thinking about God. Knitting gave me a new way of being faithful."

When the rugged individualism of the West shapes us to believe we are isolated, self-made workers and makers of our own destiny, the voices of the Black prophetic tradition remind us we are not our own. When the abstract white Jesus creates a relational ecosystem that is defined by our one-on-one relationship with Jesus, he not only betrays the wisdom of this tradition, he loses the relational focus of the Concrete Jesus.

The Concrete Jesus gives us to each other. Moment by moment God is re-creating us through each other. Story by story, God reminds us of our true identity through each other. And relationship after relationship, the Concrete Jesus invites us to reclaim our real name from God through each other.

Bell Hooks reminds us, "No one is healed in isolation."

The Concrete Jesus helps me see that savior who gave his life for us also gave us to each other. The centrality of interconnectedness and relationship in the Black Spiritual tradition guides me even deeper in my understanding of the church as the body of Christ.

Spirit does not just work through people.

God is not just present in people. But Christ is actually present as people.

TWELVE

The Meaning and The Map

Imagine there are two people who are going to trek on the same path, but are going to do so at different times. The first person has a detailed map that represents the complex features of the terrain with a high level of accuracy. Although they have never traversed this particular trail before, and do not spend much time outside in general, they are confident in their capability as a hiker because of the information they have from the map.

The second person has a significantly different background they bring to this journey. The only map they have lacks specificity in details, and compared to the map of person one, theirs is not even close to being as specific or accurate. But the defining characteristic for person two in this adventure is that they spend a tremendous amount of time outside. Their experience on various trails, and time logged traveling provides them with a high level of familiarity with outdoor terrain in general.

The beginning of person one's journey does not start off ideally. It takes them two hours to take the very first step. Their lack of experience with their feet on the ground outside trekking across unknown terrain means they have a massive barrier of fear that prevents them from beginning.

From the first step, it is clear that having a map and walking the path are not the same thing.

And as the journey unfolds, person one struggles and resists every major move they need to make to move forward and gain some kind of momentum.

When the map tells them to take this sharp turn around a cliff, they wrestle with giving up because they aren't sure if they can trust the trail. They are confronted with their fear of death with each significant movement.

When the map says to jump over a gap that is much shorter than it appears because of the false sense of depth the space creates, they almost return back to the beginning, because they aren't sure if they can trust the map or themselves.

And only 1/3 into the trail, when the path requires them to jump off of a ridge into a lagoon, they finally quit. Even though the map clearly explains that the lagoon is deep enough to survive the jump, they refuse to trust it, they don't do it, and their short lived adventure is over.

Person one does not complete the journey. And they walk back to their car defeated and discouraged. They failed to keep going, despite the comprehensive map they carried in their pockets.

As you can imagine, person two's experience is drastically divergent from person one's. There is zero hesitation when it is time to begin because their mind and body carry the wisdom and courage of all of the adventures they have gone on before.

All of the struggle and resistance person one wrestled with are replaced with confidence and fluidity. This organic movement on the trail is not because they have completed this specific trek before, but rather because they are closely acquainted with outdoor terrain and what it feels like to traverse it.

When it's time for a sharp turn, they do it. As the gap gets closer, they run toward it and jump to the other side with the kind of delight that is only possible when you know that you are safe. And as they walk toward that same bluff over looking the lagoon that forced the map expert to quit, they are so excited to launch themselves off because leaping off the edge is one of the best parts of an adventure.

And eventually, they complete the final 2/3 of the path with the same confidence and courage they began with.

And the funny thing is they never even looked at their map.

The first person understood the map thoroughly, but because they were not willing to trust the terrain, they could not complete the journey.

The second person did not spend much energy concerning themselves with the accuracy of the map, but because of their personal familiarity with the terrain and faith to trust the path, they finished this trail with ease.

Having a map of the the path and trusting the terrain are not the same thing.

And having specific beliefs about Jesus and knowing and trusting Christ are not the same thing either.

The terrain of Christ is made of trusting the divine flow, resting in grace, naturally taking sacred risks, and our ever present awareness of Spirit. Living "in Christ" is the relational and co-enacting path where our courage and the creativity of God become one.

It is the life where we give ourselves over to "love God and love another," (Matthew 22:37-39) with a great sense of passion, while simultaneously being able to "not worry about your life" (Matthew 6:25) because you know...

The birds.

(Jesus' idea. Not mine.)

It is a life that is awake.

A way of being defined by love, compassion, and courage.

The experiential knowing and embodying of Christ for our world.

And this is why I offer the map analogy. Authentic awakening in Christ and Concrete embodying of Christ can happen with our without the name of Jesus being present. You can grow in Christ without specific beliefs about Jesus.

Okay, but how does that work?

Whenever someone surrenders control and further trusts what is, they are doing the Christ journey.

Any time someone vulnerably takes a risk for the sake of love, they are doing the Christ journey.

Each moment a person chooses compassion and solidarity with the poor and vulnerable over consumption and power, they are doing the Christ journey.

Maybe you've seen someone else whose belief structure would not fit comfortably within a confessional church setting, but are compassionate, inclusive, and live with a sense of freedom and courage that appears to be so Christ-like. Like person two in that imaginative scenario, you can live on the terrain, trust the terrain, and move forward through the terrain without an accurate map of the terrain.

And in the same vein, a person can also have orthodox beliefs about Jesus and not actually grow in Christ.

You've seen this haven't you? Someone who has orthodox beliefs about Christianity and is engaged in various Christian activities, and yet they have an embodied life that does not look and feel like the essence of Christ. Maybe they have responded to the altar call and said the sinner's prayer, publicly committed their life to Jesus through baptism, and are vocal about their Christian faith—but since you are close to them, without any form of judgment of their value, you wonder, do you know any of this as a living reality for yourself?

Or what if one person is singing a song that is "Christian" and about Jesus, but is still closed off, bitter, unforgiving, and so filled with themselves they cannot allow love in?

And what if the next person is listening to different music—not about Jesus, not explicitly religious, but is open, daring to be vulnerable and honest, and has removed enough internal clutter that the healing power of the Spirit is flooding them and changing them even though they would not label their experience as a religious event?

Who really knows God? Who is actually dwelling "in Christ?"

I mean, does God actually care if you're doing "Christian" stuff, or that you're engaged in Christ-shaped behaviors and ways of being that allow grace to flow? Is being in Christ only possible when you have correct ideas about the metaphysical shape of Jesus, or does it transpire through the quality of a life marked by humility, surrender, and courage?

The Cosmic Christ cannot be contained within orthodox belief structures in the same way it cannot be contained within physical structures that have crosses on them either. Perhaps this is why G.K. Chesterton said,

"Your religion is not the church you belong to, but the cosmos you live inside of."

Now.

Let's take a deep breath for a second.

I'm with you. Are you with me?

Since we are tracking, now let's continue and explore a few stories of Jesus to see how he naturally blurs the lines between beliefs and experience, and disrupts our every day categories of in/out, Christian/non-Christian, and witness how he envisions the relationship between the meaning and the map.

In Mark 1, "A man with leprosy came to him and begged him on his knees, "If you are willing, you can make me clean." Jesus was indignant. He reached out his hand and touched the man. "I am willing," he said. "Be clean!"

Immediately the leprosy left him and he was cleansed. Jesus sent him away at once with a strong warning: "See that you don't tell this to anyone. But go, show yourself to the priest and offer the sacrifices that Moses commanded for your cleansing, as a testimony to them." (Mark 1:40-44)

What I love about this is that, on one level, it is a very simple story.

A man with leprosy—which means this is a man who has been excluded, marginalized, and outcasted—comes to Jesus and asks for healing, and Jesus heals him. Then Jesus tells him not to tell anyone (you ever heard of evangelism bro?), and to return home and honor his own traditions and practices.

What do we see here?

The power of Christ without positions about Jesus.

The substance of God without the structure of belief.

Direct experience without explanation.

This man, in his desire for healing has direct experience of the Presence of Christ without a detailed rendering of a metaphysical map about Jesus. Clearly, Jesus did not seem overly concerned with whether or not this vulnerable person believed the right things about who he was, or whether or not he got credit at all for the healing.

Which, to me, raises a profound question,

Does God need the credit in order to to be present and active?

Does the claim from the writer of Acts that "In him, we live and move and have our being" apply only to those who consciously identify with Jesus as Lord, or does this beautiful statement about union and connection extend to all people everywhere? Because if this globally unifying statement is true for everyone, then we should welcome the presence of Christ everywhere, regardless of what belief based map people are holding in the process.

Another story of Jesus that illuminates the relationship between the meaning and the map further, comes from the gospel of Matthew. Here, Jesus is talking about narrow gates, sheep and wolves, grapes and figs, good fruit and bad fruit, and cutting down trees (how can you not love this guy?). And suddenly he makes a direct and daring statement about people who are claiming his name.

Jesus disruptively says, "Not everyone who says to me, 'Lord, Lord,' will enter the kingdom of heaven, but only the one who does the will of my Father who is in heaven."

Jesus reveals the inconvenient truth that people can carry a correct map about God without embodying the living reality of Christ. In this exchange, Jesus unquestionably prioritizes walking with God, through doing the will of the Father, over claiming a name and having specific beliefs.

The Kingdom of heaven is more about embodiment than it is explanation.

The first story demonstrated that you can have the meaning without the map. This story loosens our imagination even more through inviting us to see that you can also have the map without the meaning.

This claim of Jesus echoes at all times and in all places reminding us that you can say the right name, carry the right beliefs, and engage in the right rituals, and still miss the sacred flow of Christ that is just beneath the surface of everything.

Making a distinction between the meaning and the map makes sense, but it raises a lot of questions doesn't it?

Why does Jesus even matter? Is belief in Jesus irrelevant if the Christ is already within everyone and flowing through everything? How does my relationship with Jesus actually work? What does it mean to be a mystic and still be a Christian? If you can have the meaning without the map, is there any value to the map?

Well.

To begin.

Maps are very helpful.

The intention of a map is representation. The map helps you understand where you are and what the nature the terrain you are inhabiting is like. Mapping a place out enables you to understand what the topography is like, how big a space is, and maps can give you a vision of how it all connects.

So what does a map do for our journey on the actual terrain?

It informs us and empowers us to make decisions with higher levels of intentionality. A map provides understanding of the terrain, then moves into giving us direction through the terrain. A map enables you to navigate the terrain, trust the path you are taking, and to have direction to get where you are trying to go.

(By the way, I first heard about the idea of Jesus as a map form Shane Hipps in his brilliant book, "Selling Water By the River." Although I am not directly quoting him here, that idea and book has stayed with me).

In the same way, Jesus is a map for the topography of reality. His concrete life and the nature of his relatedness to others reveals the truth of how our world works. The incarnation is a blueprint that represents the sacred pattern of everything.

By returning to a passage of Scripture about the eternal nature of Christ, we need to listen again when John says, "No one has ever seen God, but the one and only Son, who is himself God and is in closest relationship with the Father, has made him known" (John 1:18).

Previously, we saw that the phrase "made him known" is the Greek word eksēgéomai, which means to bring forth, narrate, to explain, or to unfold. If this profound concept is a torch for us today, what does it help us see about the idea of Jesus as map?

Jesus is the map narrating how the story of Divine life unfolds in and through the world.

Jesus is the map explaining who God is and how God interacts with and relates to reality.

Jesus is the map bringing forth a vision of the sacred pattern that connects everything.

And the true shape of human flourishing within the sacred cosmos is so counterintuitive, that without an accurate map, it is difficult for people to be able to see the whole truth of this configuration, and even more so, to trust this pattern.

Think about it.

Think about how absurd the map Jesus offers and embodies seems in our actual lived existence.

The way and map of Jesus says the rich and powerful are never the model for what it means to be human, and they usually don't get it. Those who desire and fight for the highest positions of status end up with nothing, and those who forgo those pursuits are the ones who will be lifted up. The religious authorities who keep trying to arbitrate who are truly in the divine fellowship are actually out of it, and all of the ones they've decided are out, are inside of it. Depth and richness in life are not found in the avoidance of our own suffering, but they emerge through compassion and opening of our hearts in solidarity with the suffering of others.

This is by no means conventional wisdom.

Oh yeah.

And losing is actually winning, the edges are the center, the lowest is the highest, and death is the key to life.

Without a map to reveal this to us and embody this for us, how many people are going to discover this, experience this, and trust it enough to know that this is the way to live aligned with reality?

Who is going to see that real power is self-emptying love for the other?

Who is going to grasp that the self that we spend the first half of our lives trying to build up is the very self that needs to die for real freedom to emerge?

Who is going to dare to look through the spectacle of the empire and see Jesus dying on the cross as the source of life?

The specific shape of "the way, the truth, and the life" (John 14:6) is so beyond what the dualistic mind can see, we need a unified map to see and behold this cosmic and concrete vision.

And if you're wondering if this metaphor is dangerous because it reduces Jesus down to an example to follow or a model to emulate, that is divorced from the living reality of Christ or the power of the Spirit, this is not the case at all. Because in practice, Jesus was not just showing us the way, he was revealing the truth, embodying the life, and continues to make a way for us to travel this path today.

Which is the entire point of having a map.

To move.

To travel.

To go on a journey.

Jesus is the incarnational map of God that co-enacts the meaning of His life by the means of our own embodiment of this life.

Adyashanti said, "So the whole Jesus story, ultimately, is the map of a journey that happens within us" (and I would add through us).

Thich Nhat Hanh wrote, "If you only satisfy yourself with praising a name, even the name of Jesus, it is not practicing the life of Jesus."

And Cynthia Bourgeault claimed that this entire journey of faith is "not just admiring Jesus, but acquiring his consciousness."

To be a Christian is not simply to believe that Jesus is the way, the truth, and the life. The gift of our existence is to travel the way, become the truth, and give the life of Christ to others, as ourselves.

Jesus is the map and Christ is the substance of meaning.

Jesus shows us the path and Christ empowers and sustains us to trust the path ourselves.

Jesus was a first century man revealing and embodying the Kingdom of God, Christ is the ever present Presence empowering us to live in this reality today.

THIRTEEN

Growing in God and The Growing of God

The Growing of God

Jonathan Edwards is one of the most famous and influential preachers in the history of the United States of America. He was a leader in the "Great Awakening," and someone who, even after hundreds of years after his death is still celebrated and reflected upon today.

He also owned slaves. One of whom was estimated to be a fourteen year old girl.

St. Bernard of Clairvaux was a 12th Century mystic that is still renowned today because of his powerful and poetic writing about the love of God. His connection with the divine was so real and his words so moving, that he was even called "the honey tongued doctor."

He also deemed Muslims as less than human, viewed them as evil incarnate, and galvanized soldiers to kill them.

There are also innumerable pastors today that have given their lives to Jesus and committed themselves to genuinely love and serve others. Leaders who mentor younger people, care for people who are sick, and carry an invisible burden for the sake of the church.

They also are vehemently anti-lgbtq+, xenophobic without realizing it, and proudly support a social status quo that continues to crush the most vulnerable people in society.

Disturbing isn't it?

Religious leaders who are connected with God and committed to Jesus still having a lens for reality that allows them to not only carry racist and sexist views, but also to remain comfortable engaging in dehumanizing behavior as a result.

What is going on here?

How can this obvious form of cognitive dissonance remain unnoticed by these leaders?

Well, think about your own life and some of the people in it.

Have you ever wondered how some of your friends or family that are kind and caring people can have such xenophobic views of immigrants? Or have you seen genuinely loving religious people, who can be so antagonistic to the suffering and oppression of BIPOC? Or have you ever been frustrated and exhausted when you see Christians lifting up the name of Jesus on a Sunday, while upholding and supporting a system of oppression and indifference Monday through Saturday?

How can people of faith be loving and caring on an interpersonal level, but still be ethnocentric, sexist, homophobic, and unconcerned about so many groups of people on a social level?

If you've asked these questions or wondered these things for yourself, you need to recognize something critical about this tension.

There is a difference between who you are and how you see.

Between spiritual experience and spiritual intelligence.

And between growing in God and the growing of God.

It is possible to be personally transformed in Christ without transforming how we see others. We can allow God's presence to make us more compassionate, while remaining in a narrow tribal consciousness that does not allow our compassion to extend to people we see as outside of our tribe. We can receive the grace of God while refusing to accept that this grace is just as accessible to people who believe differently than we do. True believers can give their lives to protect vulnerable and hurting people, but still remain unable to see the complexity of systemic oppression that renders them vulnerable in the first place.

We need Christ to transform who we are.

We also need Christ to transform *how we see*.

Imagine you are traveling up a path to the top of a mountain.

(Yes, it's another path and terrain metaphor.)

This trek has five different vistas with viewing platforms along the way. Each one of these platforms enables you to see a horizon, and the higher you go up, the depth, width, and overall expanse of the horizon increases tremendously. Between each vista, you walk on narrow trails that are blocked from the view, travel through small tunnels inside the mountain, and climb steep ridges until you eventually reach the next view.

When you get to the first view, some of the things you notice are a steep drop off right at the edge of the cliff, that none of the trees below carry good fruit you can eat, and that there is a tiny lake far off to the right in the canyon.

As you arrive at the second vista, the perceptual field is a little different. Because of the increased height and wider view, you see trees that you could

193

not see before (although the new ones still do not appear to bear good fruit), a pack of dangerous wolves in the distance, and you realize the lake is much bigger than you first imagined.

You travel further up and immediately upon the arrival at the third lookout, you are struck by the beauty of the mountain tops you can see in the distance that you were previously unable to see. You can see fields of flowers, more of the barren trees, and once again awaken to the fact that this lake is even more expansive than you previously thought.

The fourth lookout is the moment you realize a lot of your previous thoughts about what you saw were mistaken. The group of trees that you thought did not bare good fruit is actually a bountiful orchard of delicious and sustaining food. The dangerous wolves were actually just goats traveling alongside of the mountain. And once again, you see that the lake is way more massive than you ever would have previously considered.

And at the fifth and final vista, you are in awe. You see the entire body of water and it is mesmerizing. The height of your vantage point and the expanse of the horizon enable you to see the abundance of plants and animals living in harmony, and the river that runs through the environment in a unifying way.

You see all of the ways your previous conclusions based on your vantage point were misguided. The trees are good, the lake is gigantic, there is no threat of wolves, and the cliff you thought would kill you if you stepped off actually leads to a naturally inspired staircase down to the river. You also see that the beauty of these mountains is seemingly endless.

As you traveled further on the path, each horizon became wider, and thus transformed how you saw and thus, what you saw. Trees you once believed produced no life became a banquet of goodness. Wolves you saw as a threat and as enemies were transfigured into harmless goats also seeking and sustaining harmony and peace. You saw that the very same water ran though the entire region and provided for all people equally. And the step that you believed if taken would have killed you, was actually a first step toward being able to experience all of this more deeply.

So what significant things happened to the people on this path that led to such a radically new way of seeing and experiencing reality?

It was not transformation of the heart, it was the transfiguration of the eyes.

It was not that they became more, it was that they could see more.

It was not more awareness of their intentions, it was more accuracy with their vision.

This is what I mean when I mention the growing of God.

Ethnocentric religious leaders and tribal Christians are not essentially bad people, but they are stuck on a vista, and looking out of a horizon that does not liberate their imagination to see more complexity, nor permit their heart to love all people equally.

It's not that they can't love, it's just that they can't see.

It's not that their heart is incapable of love, it is that their stage of consciousness does not allow them a wide enough vision to see people they deem outside of their tribe as people who are as loved as those inside their tribe.

Just like the traveler up the mountain, our view of God, humanity, and reality is supposed to keep getting wider and more full. Following Jesus and growing up in how we see opens up an ever widening horizon that naturally leads to a vision of God that is more inclusive, and perspectives of reality that make room for more and more complexity.

We need both the direct experience of Christ within that changes who we are, and the transformation of consciousness in God that transfigures how we see and show up in the world.

Our understanding of God should be growing.

Our vision of reality should be becoming more full.

Our conception of humanity should be more and more inclusive.

We used to see the gods as angry, then we believed that anger was appeased through Jesus, now we see that God was never angry at all.

We can move from God is only with our tribe and religion, to God is for all of humanity, to God is embracing the entire unfolding universe.

We used to believe God was an object out there, then we experienced God as Spirit within, and eventually we can see God as the goal of the future we are moving toward and the depth of everything that is.

Each instance Jesus uttered the phrase, "You heard it said, but I say to you" our view of God is invited to grow. When St. Paul referred to the law as a tudor (Gal. 3:24) on his path in Christ, our collective understanding of the reality of Christ was changing. When the prophet Ezekiel imagined a future where God gives us a new heart and places His spirit within us (Ezekiel 36), he was radically re-envisioning the focus on God as external authority to inner reality.

This evolution of our understanding of God has been happening through the Bible, is still taking place today, and will continue to transpire in the future. Our vision for life is like a holy horizon that widens with clarity, includes more and more of life within its gaze, until eventually every single thing is included as a single everything.

Allowing for the growing of God in our sacred imagination should be celebrated!

We should perform rituals and throw parties when people discover that God is not angry after all. We should commemorate and re-baptize the faithful when they see that the god who has required them to painfully exclude friends and family along the way, actually includes and makes room for everyone. We should sing and dance anytime another devout seeker realizes how wrong they have been, and how much better this all really is.

We must allow God to be born again and again in our lives.

We need to refresh our understanding of who is in and who is out over and over until those categories themselves have no place in our sacred vocabulary.

We must embrace our uncertainty of belief so deeply that we eventually discover that uncertainty is the very place where true faith is born.

The Cosmic Christ is the infinite environment within which all of our finite definitions of God and life are graciously given room to live and die. And this is truly good news!

Growing in God

There is not much freedom in being a Christian without knowing Christ.

Or believing in God without being loved.

Or having faith without direct experience of the Divine.

When you have faith in God and identify as a Christian without direct experience of Christ, your religion remains, simply, a belief system. It is a set of abstract beliefs your ego holds about God and Jesus that our tradition defines as orthodox and deems Christian.

You can have orthodox beliefs about Jesus without ever being transformed by the living Christ.

But this isn't the point of a life of faith. The fullness of life Jesus named, or the freedom of the sons and daughters spoken of by Paul cannot be reduced down to cognitive certainty and loyalty to the tribe who thinks just like us.

Words like

gratitude,

awe,

freedom,

or spaciousness get us closer to "the life that is truly life" (1 Timothy 6:19).

One of the reasons these words draw us further into a path of awakening is because each of these happenings transcend the mind and ground us in our hearts bodies. You cannot just remember the concept of being grateful and recoil into real gratitude. You cannot think the experience of awe into existence, and the interior spaciousness we desire cannot simply be understood.

Waking up is more

becoming than believing,

living than learning,

and it is the moment the Word has been made flesh in your own body.

This is why when referencing the Jesus story, Adyashanti wrote, "The important thing is not what we believe about the story, but whether we have the capacity to allow it to live within us, so that the story starts to speak to us in a way that's unique to us alone." The journey of waking up transcends but includes the mind, opens the heart, and is realized through the body.

The growing of God is about spiritual intelligence, growing in Christ is about spiritual experience.

The growing of God is about how we see, growing in Christ is about who it is that is doing the seeing.

The growing of God is about understanding, growing in Christ is direct and embodied realization.

Paul said, "We are a temple of the Living God." (2 Cointhians 6:16). And Jesus invited his followers to trust that "The Kingdom of God is within you." (Luke 17:21).

Direct realization of the truth of Christ is what becomes embodied wisdom. Personal experience is the only thing that allows you to be in awe of the miracle of breath itself. Intimate knowing and being known by Spirit grounds you enough to trust that silence is actually the sound of love. Your own awareness is the only space that you can inhabit the fullness of Presence in the Eternal Now.

And if you read that and a bit of frustration sets in because you can't fully get it...

yes.

Of course.

That's the thing.

We cannot "get it" conceptually because authentic and embodied experience of the divine always transcends our mind and cognitive capacity. Direct realization does not deny the life of the mind, but it does go deeper and beyond it.

The mysterious and embodied nature of spiritual experience is what makes this path both beautiful and maddening. How do you speak of that which cannot be said? How can I conceptualize that which by its very nature refuses conceptualization? How can we use the tools of language to point toward that which transcends the scope of linguistic possibilities?

Kind of maddening right?

Recently, someone I know was preparing themselves to take an emotional risk and practice a degree of vulnerability they had never done in their life. It was going to take the form of confession and radical honesty. Before going into the defining conversation, they texted me and said they were having a hard time wrapping their head around trying not to control what happens after.

Can you relate to that?

Choosing to be totally honest, while surrendering your normal propensity to manage and control.

I responded by letting them know that this act of vulnerability and surrender is not primarily something you understand, make sense of, or grasp. Rather, it is something that has to be embodied and lived out.

The truth of the experiential nature of my friend's vulnerability and surrender is also true for direct experience of Christ. It has to be known and directly realized through the texture of your own heart and the irreplaceable location of the holiness of your own life.

But.

The good news.

Once you start to taste it, experience it, and know it for yourself.

You get it. You see it. And you know how to keep going.

As you consciously experience your true self, receive love, and know the life changing reality of being Known, it becomes laughably clear that belief and direct realization are not the same thing.

You collapse into the Self that is beneath and beyond what you always assumed was your self. The belief system that was once the home for your false self becomes a set of beliefs you have and hold, but always remains at a distance. God transitions from something you believe in with your life to something you experience as your life and feel moving through your life.

Faith as a belief system requires us to hold on to our beliefs, which means we actually are the ones in control. This holding onto beliefs is a grasping energy that constricts, tightens, and coils up.

This is why belief is easy but does not change us.

But faith as a journey of growing in Christ invites us to let go of anything that is getting in the way of the free flowing of love, which alone has the power to ground us in Spirit. Growing in Christ is a surrendering and a constant allowing that requires us to let go of the illusion of control that has been hindering us since we first held her hand.

This is why waking up is hard but transforms us.

There's a story about a group of friends that were hiking to a waterfall in Hawai'i. While they were talking, laughing, and having the time of their lives on the initial trek to water, one of the friends was having a hard time enjoying because they could not stop looking at the map.

They were checking the map incessantly, worried about losing their way and anxiously trying to keep the group on the right path. Of course, along the way, they could not recognize how much their obsession with the map prevented them from entering into the joy of the present.

And when they finally arrived at the waterfall, one of the friends grabbed the map and jumped off of the waterfall and into the water while still holding it. With a deep sense of frustration, the map keeper yelled out, "you ruined the map!"

The friend floating and smiling in the water playfully responded,

"Who cares? We're already here."

The map and directions are no longer needed when you have arrived at your destination and are swimming in the water. And although the directions analogy does not work as a whole in this context, it does create a clear distinction between spiritual intelligence and spiritual experience.

The map is not the same experience.

As your life transitions from belief in God to the lived reality in Christ, your focus and attention on the spiritual path changes.

It is not do you believe that divinity and humanity came together in Jesus, it's do you trust the union of divinity and humanity within you?

It is not do you believe Jesus was born in the manger two thousand years ago, but do you allow Christ to be born within every dark and disowned place within you?

It is not do you believe in the life, death, and resurrection of Jesus, it is are you trusting the Christ pattern of life, death, and resurrection in your own journey?

Which is why Adyashanti wrote, "The Jesus story reads like a roadmap for spiritual awakening."

Waking up and growing in Christ are the same thing.

Waking up is like moving out of a room into a bigger house, followed by stepping out into a wide open field, and eventually discovering your true home is the universe itself. The interior awakening movement is so expansive, it feels like you grow into a bigger and bigger body, until you breathe as and move with the cosmos itself as your body.

You process through this ancient future passage where your sense of self keeps expanding and becoming more free.

The concrete result of this direct experience of and sustained union with God is named clearly and brilliantly in the Bible itself as "love, joy, peace, forbearance, kindness, goodness, faithfulness, gentleness and self-control." (Galatians 5:22-23)

Paul actually refers to these qualities as "the fruit of the Spirit."

What is the organic outcome of those who know Spirit for themselves and are on a path of waking up?

Love.

Joy.

Peace.

Forbearance.

Kindness.

Goodness.

Faithfulness.

Gentleness.

And self-control.

The only fruit of authentic God experience and growth in Christ is transformation.

Besides the fruit of the waking up in the Spirit that Paul so named thousands of years ago, do you know what is natural fruit that is born out of awakening?

A return to playfulness.

Playfulness is the light hearted and relaxed enjoyment that knows that all of the pain in our world is still held in a container of goodness, filled with the substance of beauty, and grounded in something true.

This playfulness is not the ego centric, pre-rational, childish naïveté of a kid.

Not even close.

It's is the cosmic-centric and trans-rational wisdom of the adult that is awake and in on the cosmic mystery.

Here, we find our place in Chuang Tzu's invitation to the palace of nowhere, where we discover that there is no palace, and that what we seek is everywhere. We can finally sit down and relax in the temple of nothingness, because the temple is within our own hearts and nothingness is the very site we find everything. And we re-discover our voice and sing at the top of our lungs in the cathedral of emptiness, because the entire cosmos is our cathedral, and emptiness is just another name for fullness.

Waking up is returning home.

Waking up is falling in love.

Waking up is being wonderfully undone.

Amen.

OUTRO

"Will you give up public Christianity for God?"

This is a question I wrote down in a journal on January 1st, 2025 while I was spending time reflecting and seeking clarity for my future in the woods near my home in Honolulu (yes, Oahu has woods).

To give a little bit of context, this season of my life I've been feeling pretty uninterested in having conversations about Christianity, religion, and especially about deconstruction.

I know it sounds weird to hear, but a big part of me is tired of talking about God.

I told a friend this recently over drinks around Christmas, and they hilariously responded by asking, "Isn't that all you've ever talked about?"

And to add to that weakening to desire to talk about God, my relationship with public Christianity has been changing.

Don't get me wrong, between the writing and the small amount of public speaking I've done the past few years after we closed down our church, there is definitely substance and value I believe I have contributed. I have written books that I love and believe in deeply, have continued to offer wisdom through various mediums, and have done work that I am proud of.

Yes to all of that.

But if I am being honest, one of the engines that powers my continuous attempt to make a place for myself in the halls of public Christianity is quite simply, my ego.

That little part of my ego that wants to be included in a special group of people.

That little part of my ego that still wants to be viewed as unique and different.

That little part of my ego that fears being seen as "regular."

While I can look at what I've contributed through public Christianity the past few years as good, I am also aware of the ego desires at work in this pursuit.

(One thing to know about the desires of the ego, is that even after you have transcended them to a degree, they continue to re-emerge with new disguises on again and again.)

So, although ending a book about God and Jesus by saying I am tired of talking publicly about God and Jesus is of course, ironic, for me it feels like a new form of faithfulness.

This entire book is me saying that Christ is about direct experience, and following Jesus is about embodiment. And the truth is that neither one of these requires abstract beliefs and specific words, or public platforms and a following in order to be realized in their fullness.

And I am sensing God inviting me to trust this in an entirely new way.

I recently stepped into the role of chaplain for hospice care, and I love it. Through my time doing this, one of the wonderful things I have realized is that this work offers almost me everything I have ever wanted pastorally, but without any of the attention or recognition that my ego seeks in public Christianity.

My new role is a perpetual invitation to further become everything I write about in this book.

So will I give up public Christianity for God?

Well.

If trusting the Cosmic Christ is truly as good as I say it is in this book, and the following the concrete Jesus is the real path to life...

...let's just say I'm trying.

To contact Kevin Sweeney for speaking engagements,
please visit www.kevinsweeneynow.com.

Many Voices. One Message.

quoir.com

www.ingramcontent.com/pod-product-compliance
Lightning Source LLC
Chambersburg PA
CBHW071725120626
46550CB00002B/386